Straining at the Oars

Straining at the Oars

CASE STUDIES IN
PASTORAL LEADERSHIP

H. Dana Fearon III

with

Gordon S. Mikoski

William B. Eerdmans Publishing Company

Grand Rapids, Michigan / Cambridge, U.K.

Published 2013 by
Wm. B. Eerdmans Publishing Co.
2140 Oak Industrial Drive N.E., Grand Rapids, Michigan 49505 /
P.O. Box 163, Cambridge CB3 9PU U.K.

Printed in the United States of America

19 18 17 16 15 14 13   7 6 5 4 3 2 1

Library of Congress Cataloging-in-Publication Data

Fearon, H. Dana, 1931-
Straining at the oars: case studies in pastoral leadership /
H. Dana Fearon III, with Gordon S. Mikoski.
    p.   cm.
Includes bibliographical references.
ISBN 978-0-8028-6866-4 (pbk.: alk. paper)
1. Pastoral theology. I. Mikoski, Gordon S. II. Title.

BV4011.3.F43 2013
253 — dc23
                                    2012032135

www.eerdmans.com

Contents

[v]

Contents

Preface

A FEW YEARS AGO I met with a group of ministers who had
been pastoring for three to five years and were enrolled
in a continuing education program at Princeton Seminary.
One of them said, "Why didn't the seminary teach us the
things we needed to know?" I reflected upon the difference between my seminary education and the learning I experienced
in the church, and understood what lay behind this question.

On reflection, however, I think this is a misleading question. There are some things a seminary cannot teach. The variety of pastoral, organizational, and community demands; the
layers of congregational history; and the subtle expectations of
the congregation cannot be anticipated in the classroom. We
can't learn how to be pastors until we are actually doing the
work and living the life. The work is too complex, unpredictable, layered, subtle, stressful, surprising, and demanding.
There is far more art to be learned from experience than there
is science to be learned in the classroom.

Unfortunately, ministers are leaving the pastorate in wor-
risome numbers. The Presbyterian Church (USA) Board of

Pensions states: "Our research reveals many people choose to leave the parish ministry. Some choices are based on personal and other non-job related considerations. Some choices reflect weaknesses in our denominational gate keeping and call processes. Some choices may reflect simple program omissions because we have relied too much on on-the-job learning for our clergy. Historically, we have tended to blame our seminaries for any practical deficiencies."[1] The Board of Pensions offers several possible reasons why seminary graduates are leaving the pastorate. Some might feel the pressure from large debts incurred in college and seminary and inadequate compensation from the churches they serve. Others experience loneliness and the absence of a mentor. The nature of the work itself is often stormy, and it is possible that inadequate preparation has led to this exodus. Of course, there are also vocational reasons for leaving seminary or the pastorate. Those in seminary might discover that their aptitude and gifts call them to a different work and service. Such people should be reassured that, as laity of the church, they have a ministry other than that carried out by ordained ministers.

Another reason for leaving the pastorate can be traced to a persistent complaint heard from seminary graduates. "In seminary they did not prepare me for the pastorate." *From Midterms to Ministry,* a recent publication, documents this complaint.[2] An assemblage of pastors, teachers, and denominational administrators describe their experiences of moving from seminary to a position of pastoral leadership in a congregation. They describe a knowledge gap between the excellent scholastic edu-

1. *Report on Clergy Recruitment and Retention* (to the 216th General Assembly [2004] of the Presbyterian Church [USA] Board of Pensions of the Presbyterian Church [USA]), p. 9.
2. Allan Hugh Cole Jr., ed., *From Midterms to Ministry: Practical Theologians on Pastoral Beginnings* (Grand Rapids: Eerdmans, 2008).

cation ministers receive and the awareness, imagination, and skills needed for pastoral ministry.

It is not altogether clear that all of the responsibility for this gap can be laid at the door of the seminary. In just three or four years it is difficult for a seminary faculty to address all the unexpected challenges and inherent difficulties encountered in the pastorate. When returning graduates complain that their seminaries did not prepare them for pastoral ministry, they quite possibly are reflecting an inadequate process of continuing education.

Seminary education is an essential starting point. We cannot learn on the job without a seminary education because that education provides us with a theological, historical, and pastoral way of organizing our thought and experience. I enjoyed a rich seminary experience, and took into the pastorate both a more enlightened biblical imagination and a profound respect for Reformed theology as a frame of reference for living. In particular, it was through the words of James Muilenburg of Union Theological Seminary, the thundering voice of the prophets, that I became aware of the presence of God in the history of Israel. That theme was the map that led me through the Bible. At New College Divinity School in Edinburgh, I heard James Stewart make the fieriness of the apostle Paul come alive as the cold rain beat against the classroom windows, and I felt the promise of words written by that man whom Christ had made a "new creation." In seminary, we struggled with the mystery of Christ as Son of God and Son of Man, and then pondered the early church theologians as they wrestled with an understanding of the Trinity. In our mind's eye, we watched Martin Luther nail his theses to the church door in Wittenberg and heard him preach about the free grace of God. In the classroom, Chris Beker taught us to interpret Romans and Paul Scherer taught us to preach it. Reinhold

Niebuhr used the lessons of early-twentieth-century laissez-faire capitalism to show us the evil of avarice and examined the Cold War to illustrate the collective sin of self-satisfied piety and witch-hunting patriotism. Nor, but for the seminary, would we have sat in the Common Room at Union Theological Seminary on Sunday evenings and hung on every word as Henry Sloan Coffin spoke of the church with humor, wisdom, theological conviction, biblical insight, and pastoral sensitivity. He connected the dots between our theological learning and the pastoral situations we would likely encounter.

Once in the parish, the journey requires the help of colleagues, mentors, faithful church members, and teachers in continuing education programs who know from their own experience what it is all about. Making the connections between the seminary education and the life and role of the pastor still remains the central challenge.

If the question, "Why didn't the seminary teach us the things we needed to know?" is not the right question, then what is? A more helpful question, I think, is: "In seminary, what can we talk about that will help us minister?" I recommend exploring in seminary four aspects of the minister's life and work.

The first aspect is listening to people's stories. A course in ecclesial sociology (if it can be called that) would not only help us to appreciate that the congregation has been there longer than we have and has reasons for what it does and believes, but also could inform us about the new culture we have entered. Stories about baptisms, marriages, funerals, and the saints of the local church would reveal how that particular church was formed, responded to crises, handled conflict, met challenges, lived with failures, and grew its own solutions. Even if most of what we heard was laden with nostalgia, hints of a new mission for the church might lie in these stories. If we are perceptive, we can link the congregational tendencies to avoid the demands of the gospel with the broader culture of the nation, and point to the call of the Christian faith to take on problems that afflict so many of us. By listening, we can also learn to examine the community with a sociological mind-set. Uncovering data about housing, employment, schools, recreation, hospitals, nursing homes, police, social workers, how the church is perceived in the community — this is all the homework of a pastor. In seminary we cannot do that homework, but we can talk about how to do it. Finally, using theology as a diagnostic tool can be illustrated in the classroom. Asking how the ancient creeds explain current misunderstandings and heresies, seeing the approach of God to the women in the Old Testament, listening to the spiritual wisdom of Teresa of Ávila, learning of the challenges of Christianity in the global world — these can help us minister at a depth that opens eyes and ears to the sovereignty of God rather than providing a leadership that seeks the latest fad.

Secondly, in seminary we can talk about ways of becoming an effective pastor. What pastoral skills are useful in the sort of counseling we are likely to do? What does being ordained mean, and what do we mean when we talk about the ministry of laity? What can the world of business and charitable organizations teach us about leadership, and how does the Spirit call us to use power in the church? How important is home visitation? How do we revitalize our bodies and souls, and how do we nurture those with whom we live, and ourselves?

The third word is to connect to the souls of the people. People want to know more about God, and see their life in the context of a relationship with God. There are dozens of reasons why people are part of a congregation — from family tradition to a desire for friendships — but underneath they all want to know about God. People do not want to learn just traditional beliefs — although many want explanations for troublesome doctrines — but they want to know how God can be real. And they want to know what is Christian freedom and responsibility. What is a holy life? How does one deal with temptations? How do we die, and what is the meaning of the resurrection? How do we speak of the church in a time when people have lost trust in the institutions of society? When we come to the congregation with the conviction that the business of God is our business, how do we discover the will of God for our political, economic, and social life together?

The fourth word we can hear in seminary is the advice to reflect regularly on our ministry. Reflection can be a step to building better ministry and to a more satisfying life. As we reflect, we ask ourselves questions. What could I have done to keep certain destructive situations from developing? How can I enlist others in planning so that we have direction and purpose? If I am "running dry," what can I do? Reflection need not be done alone; it can be done with others, as part of a leadership style.

Finally, seminaries can invite pastors to lead these discussions. Experienced pastors would be enthusiastic about sharing the task of straining at the oars as they minister in the church of Jesus Christ and seek to carry out his mission. Classroom dialogues involving academicians and experienced pastors would not only open windows to the pastoral life, but would also ground theological education in the life of the church.

Introduction

Straining at the Oars is a collection of pastoral episodes that occurred as this pastor made the transition from seminary to the parish ministry. These episodes describe, first, the challenges; then, a way of thinking that integrates theological learning with knowledge gained on the job; and finally, the pastoral actions taken. The pastoral actions are meant to be suggestive, not prescriptive, and readers can imagine how they would develop their own ministries as they integrate their theological knowledge with knowledge gained in the parish.

Regardless of the quality of a pastor's seminary education, making this transition is difficult. Seminary education is primarily theological. In the local church, while continuing to learn theologically, pastors must also learn about the lives of church members, the culture of the congregation, and the culture of the community.

I was fortunate to attend three excellent seminaries: Union Theological Seminary, New York City; New College Divinity School, Edinburgh, Scotland; and Princeton Theological Seminary, Princeton, New Jersey. Following my graduation from

Union, I benefited from the excellent teaching and example of a senior pastor, the Reverend Dr. Arthur M. Adams, with whom I served in Rochester, New York, as an associate pastor. Yet, when I began my ministry in Lawrenceville, New Jersey, I encountered episodes that seriously challenged my ability to integrate my theological education with the work of ministry. In this book, I reflect on a variety of formative events that shaped my ability to approach pastoral ministry from a theological, ecclesiological, and sociological frame of reference.

A few words of personal background might help the reader. I grew up mainly in Brooklyn, New York, except for the time spent during World War II with my maternal grandparents in Aberdeen, Mississippi, when my father served as a physician in the navy. When the war ended and my father returned from overseas, my mother, two brothers, and I joined him and returned to Brooklyn. After finishing secondary school in Brooklyn, I went to Williams College in Massachusetts. I intended to study for medical school, but soon discovered my aptitude was not in the scientific field. However, as an English major, I had taken a few required religion courses. I enjoyed the course on the Bible and the one about contemporary theologians, including Reinhold Niebuhr and Paul Tillich. I also heard preaching on Sunday evenings that emphasized the grace of God for sinners, and the impossibility that we could make ourselves acceptable. The Bible, the gospel message, and theology captured my interest, and I enrolled in Union Theological Seminary in New York City. I continued with a middle year at New College Divinity School at the University of Edinburgh, Scotland; internships in various churches; and a summer as a chaplain in Yellowstone National Park.

I graduated in 1957 and became an associate pastor in the Central Presbyterian Church in Rochester, New York, under the tutelage of the senior pastor, Arthur M. Adams. His daughter, Janet, and I were married a month before I came to Lawrenceville, New Jersey, as the pastor, in 1960. We have two children, James and Mary, and five grandchildren. I obtained a master of theology in pastoral care and a doctor of ministry, both from Princeton Theological Seminary. During my forty-two years at Lawrenceville, the seminary invited me as a visiting lecturer for various courses involving administration, preaching, and polity.

The purpose of this book is to continue pastoral education by examining the minister's life and work in the local church. *Straining at the Oars* describes episodes in ministry that pastors might encounter, and for which there has been little preparation. In keeping with the story of the disciples straining at the oars (Mark 6:47-52), we pastors can be pictured as the struggling followers Jesus told to cross the Sea of Galilee. Like the disciples as they rowed through the storm, we encounter obstacles for which we are unprepared, sometimes leading us to a sense of despair. Time and time again, however, Jesus makes his presence known, joins us in the struggle, challenges the wind and waves, renews our courage and faith, and helps us reach the far shore. The storms that we encounter can include restructuring the decision-making process in the congregation, issues of baptism and marriage, involvement in community affairs, pastoral friendships in the congregation, handling criticism and conflict, revitalizing one's faith, doing church planning, among others. In this book we shall describe ways of sailing through opposing winds and tumultuous waters.

This book is written for seminary students who are considering congregational ministry and question what lies ahead. This will introduce them to likely situations and encourage them to ask how to integrate their seminary education with their education in the pastorate. Second, it is written for pastors early in their ministries. The hope is that they will ponder this approach of considering the interplay between their theological knowledge and the general culture inside and outside the church; be aware of the special characteristics of each pastoral situation; bring their own theological knowledge to bear as a means of filling the gaps of their ignorance; and critique their ecclesiological methods of leadership. Third, seminary professors can use this book as a way of thinking about the pastorate and use this material to present situations for study in the classroom. Lastly, church members can read this to gain more knowledge about the life and role of a pastor, and the challenges that church leaders might be called to meet.

One early reader of the manuscript urged me to "reveal my feelings." I think that I have done that where my emotions were important to the story; I also think this book is about getting results. Problems are presented, possible approaches are considered along with their consequences, and results are reported. This is not an autobiography, nor the diary of a pastor. It is a book about problems encountered in the first years of ministry, reflections, and steps taken.

One theme in particular emerges in these chapters about the challenges that are faced: the ministry of laity. The ministry of the laity involves the mutual role of the pastor and laity in confronting the storms and taking responsibility for rowing the boat. "Mutuality" is the key word and indicates recognition that the Spirit has called both the pastor and the people of the congregation to face the storms that threaten the church. The church in the Presbyterian tradition is constructed in an orderly manner, but it is not hierarchical, with the minister doing the important work and the laity following his or her commands. In the Presbyterian tradition both pastor and lay leaders are responsible to the Lord Jesus Christ, who has the power to renew people's faith and to calm the storm. This mutuality should not threaten the self-esteem of pastors as lay leaders take on major responsibilities in leadership. We can be delighted that various ministries of the church will multiply, and more and more rowers will bend their backs to pull the church forward.

The roles of the pastor are still essential: proclaiming the Word, "afflicting the comfortable and comforting the afflicted," encouraging a theological perspective of the work of the church, moderating leadership bodies, encouraging others to discover their gifts from the Spirit, encouraging vision making, and looking for that figure in the mist who, in reality, is our Lord and Savior.

Again, this is not a case of "here's how to do it." Rather, it is a review of various challenges, and possible ministries that can be undertaken by those who face similar challenges. To facilitate consideration of alternative forms of pastoral leadership, we have included discussion questions at the end of each chapter.

With the exception of the names of my family; the African American community leader Fred Vereen; Harry Kihn; Pastor Luc Deratus of Haiti; and Jim McCloskey of Centurion Ministries, all names are fictitious.

I am deeply grateful to my wife, Janet, and children, James and Mary, for their support and encouragement in these years of ministry.

DISCUSSION QUESTIONS

1. *In what ways might the metaphor of "straining at the oars" aptly capture the challenges and dynamics of making the transition from seminary to pastoral ministry?*

2. *What other metaphors might you use for the transition from seminary to pastoral ministry?*

3. *Name three or four challenges involved in the transition from theological student to pastor of a congregation.*

Acknowledgments

Professor Richard K. Fenn and I began what was, for me, an important friendship when we taught together at Princeton Theological Seminary. The courses we taught were fueled by delightful weekly lunches during which he encouraged me to tell stories of my ministry and then put them in the form of a book. But that was easier said than done, and it took years for me to shape them so they would illustrate my conviction that we pastors needed help in integrating our theological education in our work. Dick gently persisted in urging me to give it a try, until finally I made a start.

Which leads me to my second word of gratitude. The congregation of the Presbyterian Church of Lawrenceville, New Jersey, accepted me as a young minister in 1960, and welcomed Janet and me into their homes and lives. I am also very grateful to many staff members, including, among others, the Reverend Mr. Rick Thyne, the Reverend Joan Priest, and the Reverend Mac Shaffer. Also, Joan Semenuk and Jeanne Aicher, members of our core team, were a source of a constant and faithful ministry.

Acknowledgments

Living just a few miles south of the Seminary for forty-two years was a blessing. Teachers at the Seminary instructed both staff and congregation in new forms of pastoral care, worship, and education. Biblical department professors also helped me understand difficult texts for preaching.

Several pastors in the area graciously agreed to give the manuscript a first read. Among them were James Kay, Jeff Vamos, Nancy Mikoski, President Thomas Gillespie, Dave Davis, Dennis Olson, Michael Brothers, and Dayle Gillespie Rounds. Their thoughtful comments were invaluable. Friends Aristedes Georgantas and Elizabeth Christofferson assured me that the material was also helpful for a layperson's understanding of ministry.

Still more reshaping was provided by Dr. James Armstrong of Princeton Theological Seminary, who suggested ways of turning the text from simply reflection into a teaching instrument.

I was fortunate that Professor Gordon Mikoski worked with the text and brought a pastor's eye for stories that needed telling, an editor's facility with the text, and a teacher's ability to shape questions for discussion in the classroom or the local church. We used the manuscript as we taught together for two years, and we learned as our students made useful comments.

On a more personal note, I am profoundly grateful for my wife, Janet, who shared these years in ministry, and acted as a careful listener and perceptive sounding board.

Truly, writing such a book is a corporate effort that includes the stories of faith and commitment given by those who have gone ahead into the everlasting love of God.

CHAPTER ONE

Baptizing a Baby Who Has Died

S HOULD A MINISTER baptize an infant who has died at the
moment of birth? In seminary, I learned that Reformed
theology states that in such an instance it is not appropriate to
administer the sacrament of baptism. But what should a minister do when the grieving parents want their baby baptized?

Early in my ministry in Lawrenceville, I had to face this dilemma. Dan, a church member, called from the hospital in the
early morning hours to report that his wife, Lucille, had given
birth to a baby boy, but that the child was not expected to live.
Dan asked me to come to the hospital at once. When I arrived,
the nurse told me the baby had died. Entering the room, I saw a
small bundle in a crib next to Lucille. Even though the little
boy had died, Dan and Lucille said they wanted the baby baptized as Daniel Jr. Reformed theology held that such baptism
was not necessary to secure God's love for the child. I told them
that God adopts our babies before they are born and promises
to be their God forever.[1] I asked why they wanted Dan Jr. bap-

1. John Calvin wrote, "Infants are not barred from the Kingdom of

tized, as the child was already with God. They looked at me with shock and anger. From their reaction, it was clear that they believed their little boy would not go to heaven unless the sacrament of baptism was administered. I hesitated because I was afraid that administering the sacrament would reinforce their belief that we had to appease or beseech, or manipulate, God, for the sake of Daniel Jr.'s future. They were confused and angered by my hesitancy.

In that moment, it was clear that my explanation about God's love for their child was inadequate. They wanted the comfort and assurance they believed baptism would guarantee. I asked a nurse to bring a small container of water. I read a Scripture about Jesus and children, and about his love for us. Then I baptized Daniel Jr. and told them I would visit when Lucille returned home. Largely because of the pathos of the moment, I administered the sacrament. I hoped that administering the sacrament would be an instance of grace for them, helping them to believe in the care of God even in this moment.

John Calvin approached the baptism of infants with the tenderness of a parent. He wrote, "God declares that he adopts our babies as his own before they are born when he promises that he will be our God and the God of our descendents after us."[2] Calvin and his wife had experienced the death of their own newborn son, and his words are even more poignant in the light of that tragedy. His understanding of the destiny of children who have not been baptized before death echoed my conviction about God's free gift of love. Daniel Jr.'s belonging

---

Heaven just because they happen to depart the present life before they have been immersed in water." John Calvin, *Institutes of the Christian Religion*, trans. Ford Lewis Battles (Philadelphia: Westminster, 1960), 4.15.22.

2. Calvin, *Institutes*, 4.15.20.

to God is an act of God's love and is not dependent on the administration of the sacrament as a mechanism of salvation.

Soon after, I visited Dan and Lucille, and we talked again about that sad morning. I tried to reassure them of God's love and their baby's place in the kingdom. Yet, so ingrained was their fear of damnation or at least the loss of salvation without baptism, that their anger and fear were not reduced by my explanation.

On reflection, I think I should have trusted my initial instinct to provide ecclesiastical comfort rather than offer a theological explanation. I failed to realize that the correctness of my theological viewpoint was irrelevant. This couple wanted the reassurance of God's love for their dead child and were looking for the proper ritual that would speak to their sorrow and reassure them of their child's safety. They were not in a position to hear the truth about God's already-given love. When I finally agreed to administer the sacrament, it was because I belatedly realized that the dictum not to baptize dead infants — while a truth that the Reformed tradition has inferred from the gospel — at that moment was secondary to their need for a ritual that stood for God's love and protection.

Another lesson I learned in this instance is that the pedagogical dimension is wrapped in the pastoral role. Before pastors express "answers," they need to identify with those who suffer. Acknowledging suffering precedes correct teaching. What I took away from this sad event was an awareness that people would first of all want their pastor to share their sufferings; only later would they welcome a theological truth. This calls for an adjusted view of ourselves from that absorbed in seminary. I was no longer a student who brought correct answers to difficult situations; now I was a pastor and priest who was expected to minister with evidences of God's love.

A few years later Dan and Lucille indicated that they

wanted to transfer their membership to another church because they had friends in that church. That might well have been true, since the Lawrenceville church had an overwhelming number of new members. Some of the grown children of "old-timers" were leaving to join a church that was not experiencing such growth. Yet, I wonder if they were looking for a minister who personified the priestly role, a minister who lifted up their loss and sorrow to God in prayer and beseeched God to have mercy. Were they looking for a ritual that assured them that the sacrifice of God's Son opened the gates of heaven for their homeless child?

Part of the challenge in leaving the shore of seminary is to understand our new identity. A person of the academy acquires knowledge, challenges traditions, and develops new ideas. A pastor represents God to the people, and the people to God. An important task for new pastors is to learn the language of faith that the congregation speaks and to discover what the symbols of the faith mean to the members.

Discovering the meaning of religious symbols and acts will be increasingly difficult as people join our churches who come from different traditions or whose religious education has come only from watching Hollywood movies. In such critical moments as this, perhaps the best pastoral response is to ponder the tasks of both pastor and teacher, and decide which comes first.

DISCUSSION QUESTIONS

1. *What is your theological understanding of the status of babies who die prior to baptism?*

2. *Under what circumstances, if any, would you baptize a dead baby?*

3. *How much teaching should there be in the moments of pastoral care? How much pastoral care should there be in teaching?*

CHAPTER TWO

Hard Questions about Prayer

WHEN I WAS a new pastor, questions about prayer surfaced as I made hospital visitations. Do we pray only to comfort the suffering person? Does prayer actually avail us of resources that only God can provide? If we increase the number of people praying, does the larger number improve the patient's chances? In short, what is the power of prayer?

Early in my ministry, I realized that I did not have a theology of prayer. I assumed it was important to pray for someone, but did not know why. I cannot recall a seminary course that dealt with prayer, but in the hospital questions were appropriate and some sort of answer was necessary.

In the first week of my ministry at the Lawrenceville church, I received a call from a member, Miriam, whose husband, Harry, was in the hospital. She told me that during his annual checkup a growth had been discovered and he had been admitted for an operation. Upon arriving at the hospital, I heard the doctor and nurse talking to Harry. I waited in the hall, reviewing what I would do when I saw him. When the medical people left, I went in and talked to Harry and Miriam.

She was trying to be hopeful; he was clearly upset. I seconded her expression of hope without assuming certainty, and tried to share his concern. Before I left, I offered a prayer reflecting our need and asking God to help Harry recover.

What did I believe about the prayer I had just offered? I had to dig into the question of prayer. I began a study group in the church both to pray and to talk about prayer. We turned to the Scriptures, figuring there were reasons, based on experience, that the men and women of both Testaments prayed. We studied the way the psalmists prayed. They thanked, glorified, confessed to, and implored God for help, and even insisted that God heed their prayers — calling down the anger of God upon the enemies of the nation. They expressed their doubts, "My God, my God, why have you forsaken me?" (Ps. 22:1). We studied Jesus and prayer, noting that frequently he went off alone to pray (Luke 9:28), and also told his disciples that only prayer and fasting could cure certain illnesses (Matt. 17:21). He prayed for help when he faced his own death (Matt. 26:36). The apostle Paul, too, prayed. He thanked his fellow Christians in Corinth for their prayers when they heard that he was in danger of losing his life (2 Cor. 1:10). We looked at the historic prayers of the church, the testimony of men and women in every century, all inspired by the faith that there is a God who hears and responds.

The conversations of our study group led us to believe that prayer is effective at several levels. On one level, it opens the one who is praying to a relationship with God. Whether we are angry with God, or thankful to God, or casting ourselves upon God, prayer has brought us back to the Father and Mother of us all. A second level involves the person being prayed for. That person is not alone, and is assured there is a community "pulling for" health and salvation. The psalmists seem to pray on the assumption that prayer is even more effective when the community is joined in the effort. Perhaps we did not understand the divine dynamics of prayer, but we believed this was the Scripture's witness.

Why does it seem that so many prayers are not answered? The study group recounted incidents of friends who recovered, and they wondered if those prayers had been answered, but others in the group remembered prayers that seemed to go unanswered. The group arrived at a provisional explanation. They did not believe there is any way of proving that prayer "works," but there is a suggestive way of framing prayer as part of an overall confession of faith in God. God calls us into partnership or stewardship of which prayer is a part. This partnership with God involves standing beside Jesus, who prays for us, and joining him in praying for all of God's creation. Our praying recognizes the solidarity of God with us expressed in Jesus Christ. Faith in prayer is undergirded by faith in God's act of reconciling us to God's self.

More recently, I read Theodore W. Jennings Jr.'s *Transforming Atonement: A Political Theology of the Cross*, in which he describes the cross as that act in which we are reconciled to God: "The suffering and death of the Messiah place him in solidarity with the vulnerability and mortality of creaturely being. The recognition that God is fully present in the suffering and death of this one means that God has taken on the suffering and dying of creaturely existence."[1]

We are encouraged to pray, then, in the faith that God has joined in our vulnerability and accompanies us in our dying. With this faith, a pastor can enter a hospital room with the confidence that he/she brings "good news" even in life's tragic moments.

---

1. Theodore W. Jennings Jr., *Transforming Atonement: A Political Theology of the Cross* (Minneapolis: Fortress, 2009), p. 139.

It was not long before members of the study group formed a smaller group that would regularly offer intercessory prayers for the congregation. Every Sunday they gathered by the communion table following worship to pray for those whose names had been brought forward.

This corporate effort to gain knowledge about prayer shaped my theology of prayer and ministry. I could continue as a pastor with a sense of authenticity because I had something to offer: the news of God being with us, as evidenced by the cross Jesus took upon himself, joining us in our sufferings and lifting us with him to the Father and Mother of us all.

DISCUSSION QUESTIONS

1. *What is your understanding of the purpose and the effect of prayer? Do you pray to influence God in some way? Or do you pray in order to render yourself and those for whom you are praying more open to the presence and will of God?*

2. *How might the practice of ministry reshape your practice and understanding of prayer?*

3. *In what ways might prayer shape or reshape your theological understanding?*

CHAPTER THREE

Teach Us How to Pray

A FRIEND IN SEMINARY returned after spending a summer in a Benedictine monastery. He discovered this was not his calling, but he did tell us about the community's life at prayer. He told of praying in the early morning, at midday, and in the evening. There were also other hours of prayer. He said it was often a painful discipline, but there were moments when he was humbled and filled by the presence of the unseen God.

If we pastors are to pray, we need a discipline that will both feed our prayer life and call us to prayer even when we do not wish to pray. Without a discipline, other tasks are more attractive or more demanding. And when moments to relax come, it takes discipline to renew our wellspring for prayer.

Three aspects of praying assist in laying the foundation for a prayer discipline: recognition, confession, and partnership. Praying recognizes the fundamental fact of our existence. A religion teacher in a private school taught a course by asking the students "to whom did they belong and what were they called to be." Generations of students said this was a moment of recognizing they had a choice to make: Did they choose to believe or not to believe in God? Prayer both acknowledges the reality of God and initiates our life with God.

Prayer is about truth telling; it is confession. To whom are we likely to tell the truth? If we tell the truth to a living person, we run the risk of incurring blame or causing disappointment. Far too few people believe that Jesus seeks to help us, not condemn us. Far too few realize that Jesus represented God and acted for God. When we tell God the truth, especially if we accompany our telling by reading the stories of Jesus helping people who were lame or sick or outcast, a new beginning will seem possible.

Prayer is also an act of asking for partnership. We believe God is good. We also believe God works through people to accomplish that which is good and right. God created us, and fashioned us so that we need one another. God speaks to us telling us to help our neighbor, pray for our friend, offer love and discipline to our children, and extend hospitality to strangers. God's commitment to partnership with us is God's way of saving humanity and the world. When we say, "We are praying for you," we cooperate in the work of God.

Even the silence of God can be a sign of God's claim upon us, and our partnership with God. I did not understand this until I became sick enough to wonder if I would live. I prayed and heard only silence. Then I realized that my possible death, while momentous to me, was an event that happened in the care of God. The silence was God's way of telling me that even death is experienced in the presence of God. This assured me that God was doing all that could be done through those who cared about me. It was up to me to fight as hard as I could.

Discipline is necessary lest we forget to pray and forget how to pray. We can be helped by methods of praying. The first method involves a running dialogue with the Spirit, usually in solitude, accompanied by a pondering of what is happening in one's life. While taking a walk or gardening, one can recite verses from psalms and listen for an inner voice. New perspectives occur and alternatives spring to mind. For instance, one might pray, "Give us this day our daily bread," and then realize that we have already received bread that we overlooked. Hence, we are already fed and have forgotten the blessings of health we enjoy. One might pray, "Lead us not into temptation," and then realize that we are embarking on a dubious venture that will not stand scrutiny in the presence of the Lord. Familiar phrases can open the mind to unexpected words for pondering.

The second way of praying is more formal. Books of prayer from different traditions, such as the *Book of Common Prayer* (Episcopal) and the *Book of Common Order* (Church of Scotland), as well as the *Book of Common Worship of the Presbyterian Church (USA)*, prove useful. Formal prayers not only enlarge individual prayers but also introduce us to the "mind of Christ" as the church has understood it. A prayer of blessing focuses our attention on the grand issues of life: "creation," "preservation," and "love": "We bless thee for our creation, preservation, and all the blessings of this life; but above all for thine inestimable love in the redemption of the world through our Lord Jesus Christ, for the means of grace and the hope of glory."[1] Our hope is restored in spite of all that has gone wrong in our lives, in the lives of others, and even in the world.

Prayers of confession teach one how to think of humanity's frailties and misdeeds:

1. The General Thanksgiving, in *The Book of Common Prayer* (New York: Seabury Press, 1979), p. 58.

Almighty and most merciful Father, we have erred and strayed from thy ways like lost sheep, we have followed too much the devices and desires of our own hearts, we have offended against thy holy laws, we have left undone those things we ought to have done, and we have done those things which we ought not to have done. But thou, O Lord, have mercy upon us, spare thou those who confess their faults, restore thou those who are penitent, according to thy promises declared unto mankind in Christ Jesus our Lord; and grant, O most merciful Father, for his sake, that we may hereafter live a godly, righteous, and sober life, to the glory of thy holy Name. Amen.[2]

The traditional prayers of confession are vehicles of Christian wisdom, and express the deepest joys and sorrows of thoughtful Christians of the ages, bringing a broken humanity before God for restoration.

Prayers of intercession remind us of the plight of those we are inclined to forget or ignore: "Prisoners and captives, the homeless and the hungry, and all who are desolate and oppressed."[3] Remembering them brings to mind more contemporary but ignored victims, such as young girls taken into slavery, or those wandering the city streets as prostitutes. Often prayer is but the first step leading to the organizing of Christian resources into a mission of liberation.

Clergy and laity both need spiritual disciplines as a means of receiving God's grace. Practicing spiritual discipline not only consists of making oneself accountable to a group, doing Bible study, and reading meditations, but also consists of seeking solitude, silence, fasting, and service. Weekend retreats

2. The General Thanksgiving, p. 62.
3. The General Thanksgiving, p. 151.

[13]

for the laity help people rediscover the wellsprings of faith. Some retreats give participants an opportunity to share questions and convictions. Others are dedicated to silence and quiet walks along a seaside cliff. Groups of laymen and laywomen often meet weekly for prayer and Scripture reading before going to work. Many pastors seek out spiritual directors who help explore their relationship with God, each other, and all that lives.

Discussion Questions

1. *Describe your current practice of prayer. Are there any changes you wish to make to this pattern?*

2. *How would you describe the relationship between formal, professional prayer and informal, personal prayer in the life of a minister?*

3. *What other spiritual disciplines or practices have you found useful for sustaining and nurturing your faith?*

CHAPTER FOUR

Making Waves

B EFORE LEAVING Rochester to begin my ministry in Lawrenceville, I asked my mentor what I should pay most attention to during the first few years. He replied, "Work on your preaching, call on the congregation, and be careful about making major changes."

I followed his advice regarding preaching and visitation, but not regarding making changes. The change I made — replacing the pulpit Bible — is not specifically an issue these days, but its similarity to contemporary issues is suggestive. Today, change often involves "the worship wars" in which the pastor changes the order and style of worship.

In the first year, I decided to replace the King James pulpit Bible with the Revised Standard Version. The session approved the change, probably more to accommodate me than because they wanted a change. I thought it was important that the Word be read from the most accurate translation of the Scriptures so the congregation would better understand the Bible. I also believed that a more accurate translation would assist my preaching, and preaching was central in my understanding of worship.

In the words of the PCUSA *Directory for Worship:* "The church confesses the Scriptures to be the Word of God written, witnessing to God's self-revelation. Where that Word is read and proclaimed, Jesus Christ, the Living Word, is present by the inward witness of the Holy Spirit. For this reason the reading, hearing, preaching, and confessing of the Word are central to Christian worship."[1]

My own sense of being a minister was bound up in the act of preaching, and I attached central importance to the use of the latest and best translation of the Scripture. Making this change, however, assumed the dimensions of a minor crusade. Several members objected, saying simply that they liked the older version. One protestor said the language of the King James Version reinforced a sense of God's majesty. After weeks of hearing complaints, I arranged for forums following worship to explain how the newer version spoke with more clarity. Even with these explanations, opponents were not convinced. Their reasoning was that the importance of using the KJV was its connection to the past. Reading this venerable translation meant they were hearing the Word of the same God who had spoken to their grandparents in the festivals of the church year and in past moments of rejoicing and sorrow.

The anxiety that was raised by this change was a reflection of a general communal anxiety that I did not, at first, recognize. The congregation's immediate world was changing rapidly. Stores on Main Street, run by lifelong friends and relatives, were being closed because of competition from the malls. Strangers were moving into new housing developments, diluting the traditional experience of township neighborliness. The

---

1. *Directory for Worship,* in *The Book of Order: The Constitution of the Presbyterian Church (USA)* (Louisville: Office of the General Assembly, 2009), W-2.2001.

increasing size of the congregation meant strangers were elected to leadership roles in the church. Now, this new young pastor was changing *their* Bible, telling them they needed to understand the Word of God more clearly.

My failure to anticipate this opposition was probably due to several reasons: impatience to make changes I thought necessary; the belief that my seminary education trumped the place of tradition; and a failure to appreciate connections between tradition and spirituality. My approach was heavy on rationality and lacking in sensitivity.

A seminary course dealing with general congregational dynamics or the nature of community change or the interconnectedness of tradition and spirituality would have been helpful. When we leave the safety of seminary shores and encounter the winds and waves of our first voyage, a new kind of studiousness is called for. Our new task is to shape our theological teaching to encourage exploration rather than imposing our understanding of the faith. As we seek to understand, it is important to listen to congregants. They have been in that church far longer than we have, and in an emotional sense, it is very much "their" church until we earn their trust. People do not usually change their views until they believe they have been understood. Listening involves making home visitations. For by such visits, we learn the history of people with the church, their views about the church's mission, and their sense of spirituality. This is difficult because so many people work, but brief visits in late afternoon and early evening are possible. Some pastors make contacts via phone and digital media. Also, it is important not to spring changes on the congregation; change needs explanation and preparation. People value their traditions as vehicles of meaning. For instance, the members' children and grandchildren take part in the Christmas pageant, and changing the format of worship or the Scripture translation runs the risk of losing the emotional and spiritual meaning that links such events.

To deal with the controversy, I set aside time in session meetings to talk about the importance of the Protestant Reformation and emerging translations. In my sermons I included historical references to the role that Scripture has in our Reformed faith and witness. Even with this approach, we continued to use the King James Version for significant liturgical times such as Advent and Christmas, funerals, weddings, and the sacraments of baptism and the Lord's Supper — thus tapping into memories that deepened a sense of reverence begun years before. Gradually the change was accepted.

I am glad I made the change, but I could have done so in a way that others were not offended. I became wary of my own defensiveness and saw the need to be more diligent regarding research of congregational convictions and loyalties.

DISCUSSION QUESTIONS

1. *How soon after the pastor's installation should she begin to make significant changes?*

2. *What sources of information might a new pastor access to learn about the history, culture, and norms of the congregation?*

3. *What three strategies might a pastor employ to learn and listen to the congregation and its members in the first year of a new pastoral call?*

CHAPTER FIVE

Moving Power to the Proper Place

IN A PRESBYTERIAN church, the session — that group of men and women who are called elders, elected by the congregation to serve three-year terms — has the constitutional power to lead the church. The pastor is the moderator of the session.

When I arrived in Lawrenceville, this was not the case. At one of my first session meetings, an elder said the church school teachers would like a new curriculum and that they had made a choice. The session accepted the recommendation and told me to ask the trustees to approve the decision and make the purchase. The elders then said that the trustees made all decisions that involved church funds. Apparently, the trustees and the former pastor had reached the conclusion that the session had not been responsible in handling finances and the trustees had taken the power of the purse.

What can a new pastor, who is the moderator, do, when he or she is told that the session no longer leads the church? If the rightful duties and responsibilities of the session have in large part been taken over by the trustees, what course of action can the pastor take? This is a challenging situation, especially if the pastor is new to the congregation.

When I broached the topic of trustee power with the president of the board of trustees, he responded, "Dana, you don't have to worry about these details. You are free to work on your preaching and do your pastoral work. I will take care of the business of the church." I was soon to discover, however, that the "business" of the church really meant the leadership of the church in its mission.

What was the proper role of the trustees? Many churches have a board responsible for the management of the property. Members of the board act as officers of the corporation. In the Presbyterian tradition, they are called trustees. In each church, a board of trustees acts as officers of the corporation. Those corporate duties are the responsibility of the trustees, not the overall leadership of the congregation.

Secondly, churches often have a board to plan and supervise the mission of the church. Again, this board is called a session. The ecclesial answer is that the Presbyterian Church (USA) is a denomination with a constitution, and this document describes and arranges the mission of the church. Within this framework, the congregation is called upon to discern which members have spiritual gifts for leadership and elect those members as elders and members of the session.

Trying to right this misplacement of decision making, however, was more than an organizational issue. There are important theological issues attached to the Presbyterian ordering of power. First, Reformed ecclesiology confesses "the recognition of the human tendency to idolatry and tyranny." It attempts to reduce this tendency by sharing government. So men and women from the congregation are elected and installed to serve with the pastor as leaders of the church. If I had not challenged the current arrangement of power and decision making, I would have severely handicapped both my leadership and the leadership of a properly elected group. Further, the session (that group of men and women called "elders") is more than an administrative and legislative body. They are called to pray and study together, care for one another, and submit themselves to the leading of the Holy Spirit. Our Reformed conviction is that the church is more responsive to the Spirit when it is led, not by one person and not by the whole, but by a carefully chosen group set aside to open themselves to the leading of the Spirit. The pastor, as moderator of this group, has the opportunity to participate in the dynamics of spiritual leadership. All this was at stake in the Lawrenceville church.

I could have taken several courses of action. I could have accepted the situation, leaving the trustees to continue with the responsibilities of the session. Or I could have used the polity of the denomination to formally instruct the trustees and session on their proper roles, and taken action to restore the rightful placement of responsibility and duty. Lastly, I could have — without insisting that they adhere to the tenets of the constitution — convinced the trustees that the mission of the church would be better carried out when the session resumed its responsibilities. It was important not to engage in a battle with the board of trustees, or to alienate its president. Further, I did not want the congregation to perceive me as a young untried minister seeking power.

If I did not challenge the trustees' assumption of the session's rightful responsibilities, a conflict would have been avoided. However, the church's mission would have been impeded. The prescribed role of the session is to lead the congregation in its ministry and mission. The role of the trustees is to manage the property issues of the church, such as buying, selling, and mortgaging real property, among other, similar duties. A failure in pastoral leadership — in this case a deliberate avoidance of confrontation — would lead to a major dysfunction in the church.

The second alternative — informing both the session and the trustees that the pastor will make a realignment of power in accordance with the constitution of the church — would likely have led to a conflict between the pastor and the board of trustees. Most pastors can attest that congregations are more likely to think "congregationally" than "connectionally," and will resent the pastor's call to conform to the constitutional standards of the church.

I chose the third alternative: asking the trustees to return to the session its proper authority and responsibility. Providentially, a new member of the board who had been an elder in a Presbyterian church elsewhere agreed to help. Together, we suggested to the president of the board of trustees that the session could be taught fiscal responsibility if two trustees sat with the session at the session meetings, and if the session was responsible for the stewardship effort that brought forth the financial pledges for the next year's budget. The president agreed, and within a year the session was carrying out its responsibilities. When the president asked what the trustees would now do, we assured him that they had oversight of the trust funds and the maintenance of the nearly three-hundred-year-old building.

If possible, it seems better to use pastoral authority in a persuasive rather than a confrontational manner. Pastoral authority should be used to "build up the body of Christ, not destroy it."[1] The strategy we selected gave the president room to

---

1. The Rules of Discipline, in *The Book of Order: The Constitution of the Presbyterian Church (USA)* (2009-2011) (Louisville: Office of the General Assembly, 2009), D-1.0101.

be cooperative. Also, the work of pastoral leadership is not a task for one person. Other leaders in the congregation might well have more experience and expertise in organizational matters than a new pastor, and the pastor will do well to involve them.

There is a "back story" to this episode that suggests one reason that the president agreed to this peaceful solution. This back story began when I was first informed that the trustees were the leaders of the church, and I asked the president if I could attend a trustee meeting. When I arrived, he was serving Bloody Marys. During the meeting, one trustee accused the president of cheating the church of hundreds of thousands of dollars by acting as an attorney in the sale of some farmland that the church owned and selling it to a housing developer. It was a serious charge, and the president denied it but gave no explanation. As pastor, I visited the accuser and heard more details: the president of the trustees was an attorney for the developer, and the church sold the land in the 1930s for what, in 1960, sounded like a small portion of what the land was currently worth. Next, I visited the president of the board of trustees and heard his side of the story. First, when the property was sold, the president was a member of another church and had no connection with our church. Second, the price paid for the land was typical of what farmland brought in the 1930s, at the time of the sale. I talked with a real estate agent who affirmed the fairness of the selling price. Subsequently, I informed the trustees of these findings. I think the president was grateful that someone had clarified what had happened and had defended him in a way he himself could not have. I suspect that my role of helping to clear him of rumor and innuendo influenced his willingness to accept this transfer of power.

I realized that we needed to meet at a different time and place. Since I had helped the president resolve this dispute, I believed this was a propitious time to suggest a change. Thereafter we held meetings in the church on a weekday evening, and I was invited to attend on a regular basis. Obviously, we did not serve Bloody Marys.

DISCUSSION QUESTIONS

1. *What is the relationship between formal and informal power structures in a congregation?*

2. *What is your theology of power and authority in the church — particularly at the congregational level?*

3. *Why must a pastor attend to both matters of structure and the personal stories of the persons involved in changing the power dynamics of a congregation?*

CHAPTER SIX

The Congregation Teaches Preaching

I F A GROUP of ministers were asked who most influenced their preaching, some would certainly say a childhood minister or a seminary professor. Others might refer to courses they took in seminary or even books that were helpful. Many might answer, however, that their congregations taught them.

Various congregations taught me to preach. The first one was the people of Yellowstone Park. In the summer after my first year as a student at Union Theological Seminary, I was employed as a chaplain for the Christian Ministry in National Parks, organized by the National Council of Churches of America. I was assigned to the Upper Falls of the Yellowstone River in Yellowstone Park. I preached twice on Sundays at different locations to tourists and employees. When I was an associate pastor in Rochester, I preached perhaps a dozen times. Of course, when I became the pastor in Lawrenceville, I preached about forty-five times a year for the first several years, and then, as we added student interns and an associate pastor, I preached about thirty-eight times a year. It took all of this and more for me to learn how to preach. I often asked a group of worshipers to meet and tell me what they heard. I was often chagrined to discover that what they heard I did not intend to convey, and what I intended they did not hear. My initial sermons sounded like classroom lectures. If the purpose of preaching is to help people "see Jesus" (John 12:21), then I had much to learn.

In time, I came to believe that sermons have to answer four questions. The first is, "Preacher, what were you talking about?" I first heard this question from the people of Canyon Lodge, Yellowstone Park. A group of wranglers — itinerant young men who owned a string of horses that the "dudes" (summer visitors) rode — cornered me after worship and asked what I was talking about. Partly, they were "ragging an Eastern dude," but mainly, they wanted to understand what I was try-ing to say. One morning following the service, a wrangler said, "Preacher, I didn't understand a word you said." I tried again to explain the Pauline text. My friend didn't know terms like "the law," "grace," and "justification." Nor did the sermon seem to relate to his world. "What were you saying, Preacher?" is a question I put at the top of my list.

The second question is, "Preacher, what can you say when we are troubled?" The people gathered for a funeral service of a young boy who had drowned in the Yellowstone River taught that question. He was fishing with his father when he slipped and was swept downstream; his body was found a week later. When I preached the following Sunday, people asked why God allowed this tragedy. With its bumbling words, my sermon had to speak about God's taking our side and conquering death for our sakes. "Preacher, what can you say to us when we are lost?"

The third question I hope a congregation will ask is, "What do you want us to do?" Preachers, like William Sloan Coffin, let the congregation know what following Jesus means. That is not to say preachers should tell people whom to vote for, how much money to give, or what are the proper feelings religious people should hold. The sermon is a call to follow Christ. How we follow that call is a ministry charged to all of us. In this day of war and torture, racial hatreds, disdain for the poor, and threats by terrorists, Christ is calling us to "Love your enemies, do good to those who hate you, bless those who curse you, pray for those who abuse you" (Luke 6:27-28). How do we turn the call into our mission? Underlying each sermon is the teaching question, "What do you want us to do?"

The fourth question I would hope a congregation would ask is, "What have we learned about the Bible from this sermon?" Where does today's text fit in? Why was Jesus saying and doing this thing? If we preachers can locate the particular text in the larger story, we will be making sense of the Christian faith. People want to know what the Bible is about, and teaching the Bible is a long and involved process.

While the questions of the congregation are important, preaching itself is about asking questions. The questions flow from the preacher wrestling with the text, from the congregation's questions, and from the preacher's experiences with the "groaning of creation." Preaching is raising questions that can be answered only by turning to God and discovering both the grace and the demands of God.

DISCUSSION QUESTIONS

1. *What are the key differences between a classroom lecture and a congregational sermon?*

2. *How might one go about intentionally contextualizing one's sermons to be lived questions and problems of a particular community of believers?*

3. *By what means can pastors continue to develop their preaching effectiveness from novice to expert?*

CHAPTER SEVEN

The Pastor's Day (and Evening)

O NE OF THE MOST confusing aspects of being a new pastor is the use of time. Pastors rush from task to task,
looking for time to write a sermon, visit parishioners in the
hospitals, and attend back-to-back meetings. When we graduate from seminary and begin our pastoral work, our use of
time changes dramatically. We still run a marathon, but it is
a marathon made up of a series of "wind sprints," in different
directions.

As students, we took hours to read a book, days to write a
paper, weeks to prepare for a final. In the church, daily
events fracture the pastor's time into half hours and hours.
The tasks are many, varied, and often unpredictable: preparation of prayers and sermons, shaping orders of worship,
visiting in hospitals and nursing homes, doing funeral and
wedding services, meeting with committee heads and other
church employees, listening to people with pastoral concerns, asking people to serve in a variety of ways, greeting
newcomers, and attending evening meetings with committees. In addition, there are also the occasional fixing of

stopped toilets, mopping up flooding basements, and finding people to repair faulty furnaces.

The demands of this life present challenges involving the use of time. The first challenge for us pastors is to use time and not let time use us. That is easier said than done because much of our ministry consists of responding to unexpected calls for help. The challenge is structuring our days and evenings to allow time for accomplishing regular tasks while also meeting emergencies.

Structuring our time helps. Ministry can be viewed as having these basic tasks: communication, contact, and coordination. How much time is needed for communication, that is, for preparing sermons and orders of worship, newsletters, letters, and lessons? How much time for contacting people through pastoral visitation in hospitals or home calls or listening to cries for help that come during the week? And, how much time do we need for coordinating the work of the church and our work in the community? My experience was that about a third of my workweek was devoted to each category.

We can find time. If we keep a record for some period of time, we will discover gaps of wasted time we can fill usefully. Knowing what we need to do, and the time required to do it, makes it easier to find time to meet emergencies. During some weeks, a series of funerals will mean we spend less time coordinating the church's work. During other weeks, a rash of meetings means we have less time to spend communicating. We make compensations until we can rebalance our week or month.

The second challenge is to move through our daily schedule and various ministries with an integrated sense of self. What about our sense of self connects our various tasks such as preaching with attending a finance committee meeting or counseling a married couple, or leading prayer at a township

meeting, visiting a hospital, or organizing a housing committee? How are these various tasks integrated for our sense of being a whole person? Is there some thread of identity and purpose running through the various pastoral tasks that is both
consistent and yet allows for adaptation? The same person
does it all: What is the consistent thread?

E. Brooks Holifield, in *God's Ambassadors: A History of the
Christian Clergy in America*, cites theologian James Gustafson's
review of a minister's duties referring to the myriad of tasks
that can lead to a confused sense of self: "They were preachers,
scholars, teachers, priests at the altar, and counselors, but
they also conducted financial campaigns, managed public re-
lations, devoted time to extra-parochial church boards and
councils, assumed denominational tasks, mediated community conflicts, prayed and spoke in civic groups, cooperated
with social agencies, engaged in social reform, directed recreation, and administered 'multiple organizations' within the
congregation."[1] Reflecting on this description, Holifield refers
to the concern in the 1950s and 1960s that the clergy lacked "an
integrating conception of ministry." He writes, "Seminaries
had failed to provide them with a theoretical foundation that
united a 'theological doctrine' of ministry with a 'sociological
definition' of clerical tasks."[2]

From my theological education, I developed a perspective
that helped integrate a sense of self. My baptism signified that
"I belong to God through Jesus Christ." My ordination provided me with the integrating question for all situations,
"What is the will of God in this place where I am called to
serve?" My pastoral identity was based on the sense of belong-

1. E. Brooks Holifield, *God's Ambassadors: A History of the Christian
Clergy in America* (Grand Rapids: Eerdmans, 2007), p. 242.
2. Holifield, *God's Ambassadors*, p. 243.

ing to God and being called to serve; my tasks as a pastor sought to respond to the question: What is the will of God here and now?

The third challenge is to avoid using time to impress ourselves and others regarding our worth. In ministry there are very few legitimate markers of success. We are tempted to appraise our value by the size of our congregation or the growth of the church budget. Another tendency is to convince ourselves that we are valued because we work long hours. Again, we fall victim to time using us.

The marker Jesus applied to himself and his followers was faithfulness. Jesus told a story of the master of the servants who said, "Well done, good and trustworthy slave; you have been trustworthy in a few things, I will put you in charge of many things; enter into the joy of your master" (Matt. 25:23).

What does faithfulness look like in the pastoral life? We are "called" into ministry. We are not employees, responsible for only a limited period of time with a contract allocating our payment and benefits. We are called to be witnesses of the world's afflictions, and to proclaim the nearness of God. We are interpreters of humanity's loneliness, and we proclaim in every waking hour the sights and sounds of the Spirit at work. We are not organizers of the status quo, but we give notice of the kingdom on earth. We are not administrators "greasing the wheels," but we facilitate the work of the Spirit, strengthen the body of Christ, nurture the covenant community, and witness to the kingdom that is "already and not yet." With this sense of what it means to be called, we are in a position to use our time faithfully.

DISCUSSION QUESTIONS

1. *Either ask an experienced pastor to record daily activities for one or two weeks or keep your own time record. What do you notice about the use of time? What surprises you?*

2. *What proportion of a pastor's week ought to be apportioned to ministerial duties, family responsibilities, and personal care?*

3. *What understandings of pastoral ministry does the pattern of time usage indicate? What core values? What are the strengths and weaknesses?*

CHAPTER EIGHT

Having Friends, Not Cronies

WHILE IN SEMINARY, we were told by a professor not to have friendships in the churches we served. Presumably, he meant that the congregation would be afraid we would betray pastoral confidences or we might favor some members over others for positions of leadership. There is a difference, however, between having friends and being guilty of cronyism. The latter term, often used in a political sphere, means to appoint people to office on the basis of friendship or favor. Using the term in the pastoral context would indicate a special relationship that violates boundaries necessary for professional behavior.

The first Christmas I was at the Presbyterian Church of Lawrenceville, a member, whom I had not previously met, sought me out on a Saturday afternoon when I was working on my Christmas sermon. He said that he knew ministers did not receive much pay and wanted to give me $200 to buy presents for my children. Perhaps he was simply being generous, but I was afraid this was a bid to become a crony. He was a favorite of my predecessor, and church members reported that he regularly took my predecessor on three-day fishing trips. I was afraid he wanted a special relationship with me akin to the crony relationship he had with my predecessor. I thanked him but said I did not need the money. In hindsight, he might only have wanted to help a new pastor, but I was afraid to take the chance.

The apostle Paul, as he gathered and nurtured new congregations, cherished his friendships with people in congregations. Paul was a sensitive, proud, and quick-tempered man with a tendency to boast; yet he had a genius for friendships, as witnessed by "the extraordinary list of friends" he mentions in his letter to the Christians in Rome.[1] He wrote of those who had "risked their necks" with him and spoke of his first convert in Asia as his "beloved." He called two friends who were with him in prison "my relatives"; others he called "brothers and sisters." Clearly, he had close friends in his congregations. He made no mention of the difficulties this might have caused.

Jürgen Moltmann makes the interesting point that by his friendships Jesus brought the kingdom to those who had previously believed that they were excluded from the kingdom of God. "As the messianic harbinger of joy, Jesus brings the gospel of the kingdom to the poor and becomes the friend of tax collectors and sinners."[2] Jesus was not patronizing in his friendships — eating with tax collectors and sinners to show what a charitable person he was — he did so because they were truly friends.

Often we develop friendships in the congregation because we share our faith and affection for the church. Also, pastors and member-friends have gone through experiences that bind

1. *The Interpreter's Dictionary of the Bible*, vol. 3 (Nashville and New York: Abingdon, 1962), p. 689.

2. Jürgen Moltmann, *The Church in the Power of the Spirit: A Contribution to Messianic Theology* (Minneapolis: Fortress, 1993), p. 119.

them. They have lived together through times of joy and sorrow, and it seems normal to develop friendships.

But cronyism is another matter. It can dull the prophetic edge of ministry. There was a pastor of a church whose members were employed by a local mill. The owner gave the pastor expensive gifts, including a Christmas bonus. Most townspeople knew that the mill was polluting the local river that ran through the town, but the minister felt constrained by his friendship and did not confront the owner either personally or in his preaching. It might well be that the gift giving comes without strings attached, but it is also possible that the pastor might lose the independence necessary to preach the sharp edges of the gospel.

Sometimes members give gifts to pastors out of respect or affection, and the pastor must decide how to respond. Will a grateful acceptance convey the pastor's appreciation, or will it imply that the pastor gives special access to the donor? The general rule might be to receive gifts offered in friendship, yet not offer favors that compromise the ministry. Within those parameters, the congregation is a fruitful ground in which to grow a lifetime of friendships.

Single pastors living in small towns might find it extremely difficult to have friends in the congregation. One reported that in her first years at such a congregation, she was exceedingly lonely, worked long hours, and had little time for close friendships. To offset such loneliness, some pastors meet regularly with seminary classmates once they are settled. In some instances, it might be advisable for a pastor to seek close friendships with former acquaintances and classmates, or with groups outside the church that gather for activities such as hiking, canoeing, or singing in a chorale.

When Janet and I arrived in Lawrenceville, we wondered if others would befriend us. Months later, we discovered that church members were wondering if we would befriend them! In due time, we could discern who sensed that there were boundaries to be respected, and who wanted to cross those lines. The great majority of members respected the bounds of confidentiality. The people of a congregation want a pastor who is approachable, who will listen, take an interest in them, speak to their thoughts and aspirations, and not retreat or stand in judgment.

A church fellowship program was developed that helped members of the church to know each other and gave us the opportunity to know them. Small groups of congregants met for dinner and conversation, and Janet and I attended most of the meetings. The proximity of the pastor in social settings gave many people the opportunity to know us, and this, in a sense, demystified the person and role of the pastor. Even with these friendships, pastoral boundaries were kept in place.

There are guidelines that help facilitate friendships. First, being friendly to everyone is important. Not only is friendliness an overture to a deeper pastoral relationship, but also pastors have the rare opportunity to help people find new ways of relating to one another. The friendliness of a pastor can give a defensive person the opportunity to show a more intimate side. Second, pastors can share knowledge of the goals of the church and the challenges the church faces, thus welcoming the person into the world of the church and implying that the person's understanding and support are important. Third, if a person asks for knowledge that is protected by the rules of confidentiality, a pastor can explain that the person's question is important and reveals the person's sincere concern, but that the information has to remain confidential. Fourth, friends know there are challenges in being a pastor, and they do not ask for inside information since they want to support a friend and not make life more difficult.

It is also possible to have friends outside the church. I developed a friendship with someone I jogged with who also was the principal of a school. His work and mine bore similarities, and we talked in generalities about the highs and lows of our work. Another friend I made was a physician, not a member of the church, who understood the pressures of pastoral work and listened — even giving counsel that put frustrations into perspective. There was never any danger of their friendships interfering with pastoral duties. It is likely that most friendships involve using discretion about confidences. Pastors only need to be more aware of boundaries, and even the appearance of favoring some people over others.

DISCUSSION QUESTIONS

1. *Should pastors develop personal friendships with members of the congregation? Why or why not?*

2. *How would you articulate the appropriate professional boundaries between pastor and people in a congregation with whom the pastor feels positively disposed?*

3. *What are some specific ways that pastors can handle closer relationships with some members of the congregation without making others feel neglected or feel that the pastor is engaging in "cronyism"?*

4. *Where should pastors go to cultivate friendships beyond the congregation?*

CHAPTER NINE

Needing Help and Accepting It

E VEN PASTORS NEED HELP, but might be hesitant to ask for it. Below are three incidents in which I needed help: one was caused by my own loss of temper; one because I did not think the church could afford additional pastoral help; and one by a misunderstanding of a scriptural text I used in worship. In each instance I wondered, "How will accepting help affect the congregation's perception of me as the pastor?"

The first instance involved my loss of temper. While in my office one Saturday morning, I received a telephone call to which I could not give an answer until I had talked with my wife, Janet. She was at home in our kitchen preparing a church luncheon with other women. I crossed the driveway and entered our kitchen, then realized we could not have a conversation with others present. I returned to my office. A while later I tried again, but came back with the same result. On my third visit, I found two women still working. It was then that I blurted out something to the effect that I couldn't talk to my wife when I needed to. Insulted by my remark, the two women left immediately.

The next week I visited them. The first said she had never been so insulted in her life, and she didn't know whether or not she could return to church. She was angry because her pastor had been rude.

The second one invited me into her house and offered a glass of sherry while we chatted. She did not know what was troubling me, but she realized I needed a friendly response. This was an act of grace. I had not asked for help but she offered it. I later learned she had experienced considerable trouble and could recognize when someone needed help. This episode led me to deal with some personal issues that caused such outbursts.

Another instance of help happened when an associate pastor suddenly decided to accept a call to a position in California. It was in the spring, which is not a good season to find a replacement. Carrying out the church responsibilities without an associate was difficult, but since the economy was in a recession I hesitated to ask for help. One Sunday, a member who was aware of the staff problem asked if he could provide funds for part-time pastoral help. This was another act of grace. He also saw that I was in trouble, and he stepped forward to help.

The third episode involved a sermon I preached and the conflagration that it nearly caused the first year of my pastorate. I preached an Advent sermon based on Luke's text of the Magnificat. I spoke of the origin of the prophecy and the way Jesus fulfilled it, and then spoke of the mission of the church to follow Christ. Here is the portion of the text that caused the angry reaction:

He has shown might in his arm:
He has scattered the proud in the conceit of their hearts.
He has put down the mighty from their seat,
and exalted the humble.

He has filled the hungry with good things;
and the rich he has sent empty away.
He has received Israel his servant,
mindful of his mercy.

(Luke 1:51-54)

A member of the church who heard the sermon belonged to the John Birch Society, a right-wing political organization that compiled a list of those suspected of being communists. This member, not knowing the Scripture, called the clerk of the session and accused me of reading communist literature from the pulpit. The clerk took this accusation seriously because the member had been part of a small group that had urged the resignation of my predecessor. The clerk called a professor from the seminary who was a member of the church, told him the story, and the professor laughed. He explained it was not communist literature at all; it was the Gospel! The clerk called the member and told him what the professor had said. After I was informed, I visited the man. He quizzed me rather closely about my political philosophy, and with every statement I tried to show my reasoning as a Christian. In time we became good friends.

These members realized that even a pastoral leader can use advice, support, and help. A pastor has frailties and is part of a Christian community. We help one another. As a friend said when I told him about this sort of help, they realized that I was "set apart," but not "too far apart."

Whether we wish it or not, a pastor is often taken as an example. Others look to us pastors hoping to see what a Christian looks like. However, that does not mean we have to pretend to be superhuman. If we are tired, it is human to seek some rest, and not try to prove that we are stronger than others. If we are dealing with a pastoral tragedy, it is human to reflect the sorrow — and to share it. Perhaps some in a congregation will want us to appear to be superhuman, but most people will be grateful that we are humans who turn to God and to others for help.

However, there is a tension between carrying out the duties of the office of the ministry and accepting help. Congregations call pastors to be leaders, especially spiritual leaders. They expect that we pastors have submitted ourselves to the disciplines of the faith and can exhibit some self-control and wisdom. We are expected to draw our strength from being spiritually healthy, which includes the discipline of study, prayer, exercise, and the counsel of trusted friends. We are called to be the "servants of the servant Jesus Christ." A servant must be an able person; otherwise he or she will not be fit to carry out the work of the servant. That does not mean we cannot accept help from others who are part of the church. When we make mistakes, we can accept help, and try to rectify them without diminishing the stature of the office.

On the other hand, if a pastor needs professional help, the church should make sure it is forthcoming. Many a church has benefited from a pastor's newly discovered inner peace, increased self-acceptance, and enthusiasm for the work.

DISCUSSION QUESTIONS

1. *In what ways might pastors allow members of the congregation to minister to them?*

2. *Identify the warning signs of exhaustion, disease, or mental illness. How might you recognize them in yourself?*

3. *Where can pastors go to get help for personal and professional problems?*

CHAPTER TEN

Wearing the Collar

DOES A CLERICAL COLLAR still signify authority to the public? Years ago, wearing the collar signified that a member of the clergy stood for precepts that society recognized as having moral authority. When those who wore a collar spoke in public meetings or took public actions, they were accorded at least the appearance of a thoughtful response. Has that changed? As a friend commented, the church is no longer "the custodian of learning or the monitor of public morals."

There are still times, however, when in the course of a daily ministry a member of the clergy dons a clerical collar and identifies herself or himself as such in public in order to carry out a ministry.

Four instances come to mind when I acted as a representative of the church — wearing the collar in public — to carry out a ministry in a language that those in the public world might understand. Other pastors can, I am sure, give numerous examples of the same role they have played in the public sphere.

Beginning in 1968 and going through the tumultuous 1970s, people were rioting in the inner cities of Chicago, Detroit, and Los Angeles. Even in nearby Trenton there were rumors of demonstrations that might lead to riots. The word was that mobs would march into the "lily white suburbs," and local radio stations warned us not to enter the city. The city was off-limits to all except people with official business. At the time, I was a member of the township civil rights committee, and church members, knowing this, asked if the rumors were true. Saturday night, wearing my collar, I drove into Trenton. A few police officers stopped me as I neared the county courthouse. When they saw my collar, they asked me where I was going, and I replied that I was going to the courthouse because I wanted to find out how I could be helpful. They replied, "Okay, Father, but be careful." When I entered the courthouse, I found police standing in the hallways, dressed in riot gear, talking and laughing with African American citizens. I asked some officers if there was any trouble, or if they expected any, and they said everything was fine. Nothing happened that night. The next day, in worship, I reported the visit to the congregation and made some remarks about rumors. I had used my collar as a public symbol for ecclesial authority, at least with the police of Trenton, to enter an area restricted to other citizens. I had also offered my services, and the police apparently believed that I had the right to make the offer.

Wearing the collar and claiming an ecclesial authority to venture into the center of the rumored conflict helped me gain information. I had no agenda other than to find out what was happening; I was not making the trip to represent the rights of those who might riot or those who might be threatened. I simply wanted to know the truth of the situation, and report it to the congregation. Having made the visit, I assumed that when I told others what I had seen, I would partially defuse the mounting fear and hostility. Wearing the collar achieved its purpose; it gave passage into Trenton where I could gather accurate information intrinsic to peacemaking and reconciliation. There was a rumor that we were going to be invaded by hordes from the city, which was not true. Those in our town who were loading their guns would now be less inclined to panic. I wore the collar so that I could carry out the role of the church as peacemaker.

Sometime later, I wore a clerical collar when the chief justice of the New Jersey Supreme Court asked me to chair a committee that would review and update probation and parole procedures for the county. When I asked him why he selected me, he said it was not only because I was serving at the time on a committee that heard cases of juvenile crime, but also because he wanted a chair who was neutral and not associated with the law enforcement establishment, a political party, or a prisoner rights committee. He believed that my office as a member of the clergy stood for truth telling and fair actions. Being clearly identified as a member of the clergy was perceived as an advantage for service in a public role.

In another instance, a church member asked me to accompany her to pick up her worldly belongings from her apartment in Trenton. She was separated from her common-law husband, who had just escaped from the county prison farm, and she was afraid he might be there. I called a church member who worked in the district attorney's office and asked if he could arrange for some police officers to escort her; he said there was no official "paper" on the man yet, but he would send a couple of officers. We met the officers in front of the house, and they told us that I would have to lead them up the stairs to the apartment, as if I were visiting him, because they did not have a warrant. Because I was wearing my clerical collar, I hoped the escaped prisoner would let me talk to him. I went up and they followed — with drawn handguns. I told them that when we got to the top of the stairs, I would knock, identify myself, and then step aside. The police officers agreed. We did this, but no one was there. So we took Sandra's possessions and loaded them into my car. Again, being a member of the clergy and wearing this symbol of ecclesial authority persuaded the police to be as helpful as they were allowed to be.

A traditional role of the church is to help the poor, the powerless, and the dispossessed. The police knew I was there solely to help my parishioner, a person who had little. They apparently recognized that the church had a traditional concern and that historically the church's service has been directed to "the least among us."

Finally, a church member asked me to visit a childhood friend, a man who had grown up in the church and was now in prison. He had a history of trouble with the law, and I had visited him in jail on other occasions. When I made those visits, I wore my collar. I believe it acted as a sign of my authority and purpose, and facilitated cooperation and entry. When it came time for him to be paroled, his friend asked if I would help secure the parole. The court asked if the church would pledge to be his sponsor. I asked the session and they agreed. We pledged to be his overseer. I assured the prison authorities that the church would help him return to society, and they took my promise seriously, knowing that such an offer was within our tradition. The officials recognized that the local congregation might well be a community that could provide and be a sign of authority that this young man needed. A church family took responsibility to see that he was in worship on Sundays. Another member befriended him and spent time with him every day, listening to his outbursts of anger. When he went "off the wagon," I joined another of his friends to find him in local bars and bring him home. Even the local police, who knew his history (some of them had gone to school with him), tried to be helpful.

In these instances, wearing the collar or using the authority of the church for the traditional mission of the church was a language that people involved in the public world understood. I believe the clergy still have this language available to use in the service of the church in the public sphere.

Other pastors have been asked by church members to help them represent their case to public and school authorities. A child might behave poorly in class, yet only the parents realize it is because their child is bullied. The family asks the pastor to make a school visit, and she does so, wearing her collar. This symbol stands for the authority of the church, which has been called to serve others in the name of Christ.

When the civil rights movements were at their peak, ministers wearing the collar and marching in protest were as likely to be jailed as anyone else. In fact, some of them wanted to be jailed, they said, as they were then able to demonstrate that the church was on the side of the oppressed. This public witness by the church angered many, but the anger itself was a witness to the power of the symbol.

When we advocate for the powerless, wearing our symbol of faith and morality, and touch on ancient traditions, we remind the public that the foundations of a just society need constant maintenance. Even though the authority of the church has waned, we can still use the church's authority in the service of others. Pastors and the church are commissioned by Christ to stand up for others, especially those who are without help. Recognition of our authority has diminished in our society, but there are still ways we can reclaim and use the authority of truth, justice, and mercy in the service of Christ.

DISCUSSION QUESTIONS

1. How would you characterize the role and responsibilities of pastors in the public arena?

2. What theological, ecclesial, and personal issues are involved in clergy wearing religious symbols or clothing in public?

3. What are the limits to pastoral involvement in public witness?

CHAPTER ELEVEN

Placing the Flag

D URING THE VIETNAM WAR, several members asked that
we remove the American flag and the Christian flag from
our place of worship. They said it was a place for worshiping
God, and the presence of the flags suggested that we had gathered to worship the nation and the church. Those who wanted
the flags to remain said that removal would be a sign of national disloyalty, and a sign that we had abandoned our young
people who were serving in the military. The session was un-
able to resolve the issue with anything approaching consensus, and we did not remove the flags from the worship space.

When the interior of the worship space was painted, the
flags were removed. When the painting was finished, I told
the custodian to leave the flags on the stage in the assembly
room. A few persons asked me why the flags had not been returned, and I said the signs of God whom we worship – the
cross, the communion table, the baptismal font, and memo-
rial flowers – were the only appropriate symbols for use in our
worship space.

Several years later a family offered to donate new flags and flag stands in memory of their deceased mother. They also wanted them displayed in our worship space. I took the request to the session. They were sharply divided, and this division reflected the feelings of the congregation. Fueling the debate at this particular moment was the emotional power of a family making a gift in memory of a beloved member. This trumped the liturgical or theological argument that I made. I did not object to the decision.

The dilemma for the pastor is how to maintain the theological integrity of the church and the true meaning of worship, while at the same time avoiding a conflict that could severely split the congregation as well as jeopardize the pastor's leadership of the church. This is a conflict of values. On one hand is a theological understanding of the church as a fellowship called to worship the Lord above all other loyalties. As *The Constitution of the Presbyterian Church (USA) 2009-2011, Book of Order* states, "God has put all things under the Lordship of Jesus Christ and has made Christ Head of the Church, which is his body." On the other hand, many Christians have a strong sense of patriotism and a deep commitment to the nation. These convictions and intense feelings of loyalty are especially strong when the nation is at war and our young men and women are risking their lives in the armed forces. The flag is a symbol of these feelings. To remove it from the place of worship seems, to many members, disloyal and a betrayal.

As I made this decision, I asked myself if I lacked the courage to fight for what I believed was right. However, my hesitancy to enter this fight arose more from my conviction that my leadership depended on several factors. One factor was my desire to seek change in an evolutionary rather than revolutionary manner. I was willing to work gradually but insistently toward a greater faithfulness. Part of evolutionary leadership in the parish is education, a process of leading people from the known toward the unknown. To arrive at a new position, or to appropriate a new body of experience and knowledge, the leader has to take people across an area they do not know toward an area of new knowledge and experience. In this instance, I did not think enough people would follow me from the known area of patriotism to an unknown area of a prophetic view of the church vis-à-vis the nation.

Another factor was that I did not want to lose the congregation's confidence that I knew their mind. It was important that I understood their convictions and respected them. I led as one who preaches and teaches rather than as one who takes a heroic stand and forces others to either join or fight or ignore.

A third factor was that I had been a pastor long enough to realize that as time passes, so does the relative importance of certain challenges. In time, it is possible that we could discuss the theological meaning of this event and move the flags without a congregational split. But, if I had seriously fractured the church, it could take years, if ever, to restore the church to vitality and health. Our churches are fragile, and it does not take much of a calamity to drive them into extinction.

In pastoral leadership, it might be clear to the pastor what is the right thing to do, but it is not always clear how to do it. A pastor would like to move the church in more faithful directions, but "doing what is right" often involves challenging customs, traditions, beliefs, and behaviors that are embedded in the life of the congregation. These traits often signal deep loyalties that help people feel proud or secure or righteous. Doing what the pastor deems to be right means challenging beliefs that are central to individual and group identity. In those years, challenging the place of the American flag was threatening to some veterans of World War II, to parents of those serving in Vietnam, and to those who simply believed what was true according to the administration in Washington.

One way I have thought of pastoral leadership is to construct a provisional picture of what faithfulness looks like in this particular church and work toward that goal. As challenges emerge, the pastor will measure them against this picture, either seeing a fit or a misfit, or letting the new challenge influence the picture. Taking this longer view means the pastor evaluates reactions and responses along the lines of these far-ranging goals. Some challenges can be handled through a gradual process over some months or years. Others have to be met head-on, regardless of the controversy they raise. To not confront them would mean to lose the essentials needed to move the church toward this picture. Such instances arose in the 1960s in our area when it was essential to declare that the session must admit into membership anyone confessing Christ as Lord and Savior regardless of color. That could not be compromised without destroying the meaning of the church. The session did so, in spite of the disapproval of some leaders and members, but they knew this issue could not be compromised.

How does one measure the faithfulness of pastoral leadership? I believe that the passage of time gives the pastor and many church people a perspective on the stands they took that required courage and decisiveness. Many of those who were hesitant and only silently supportive at the time now see the role of the church as a "provisional demonstration of what God intends for all humanity." And yes, in hindsight, there were instances when it was apparent we were not as faithful as we might have been. But the challenges continue to come, and it is to be hoped that we learn to trust in the Spirit of Christ.

DISCUSSION QUESTIONS

1. *Identify three theological reasons for and three theological reasons against displaying a national flag in the congregation's worship space.*

2. *In what ways do theological, pastoral, stewardship, and personal issues intersect in issues pertaining to the use of national symbols in the church?*

3. *What strategies might you develop to address constructively major conflicts about a social or political issue among the leaders of a congregation?*

CHAPTER TWELVE

Criticisms and Conflict

A S MANY PASTORS can testify, there is no shortage of either criticism of the pastor or conflict in a church. Studies suggest that pastors are accomplished at building relationships and making peace, but are not as proficient in dealing with confrontations.

There are several reasons for conflict. First, there is a freedom in the church to criticize without fear of the sort of penalty that might be incurred in the workplace. Second, in part, religion is about accepting people, and we are tempted to use that allowance to vent our anger. Third, some of us have come from a background where a sense of identity has been achieved only through anger and attack. Fourth, the gospel is about change as much as it is about stability. When people in churches seek to change certain customs and traditions in order to be faithful to their understanding of the gospel, others resist and fight back. Often the minister is in the middle of conflicts.

What is our role as pastors in times of conflict? Our response to conflict is a form of self-offering. Others expect, and we ourselves expect, that we will be patient, kind, forbearing, and understanding. While the normal expectation is that ministers will offer themselves to bring justice and make peace, the church calls all of us to "confess our sin and complicity in brokenness, to repent, expressing sorrow and intention to change, to accept God's forgiveness and extend forgiveness to others, to work toward reconciliation, and to trust the power of God to bring healing and peace."[1]

We are called to care for one another in daily living, sharing joys and sorrows, supporting one another in times of stress, and working for reconciliation. These responses are part of the responsibility of any Christian.

Certain strategies are helpful in extending this care to others. To deal with personal attacks and complaints, I developed a series of instructions for myself, written on a card that I kept near my telephone. The card read: "Get Explanations, Clarify the Complaint, Work for Resolution."

Get explanations. If I was criticized, I would acknowledge how the person felt and let the person express whatever feelings were involved. For instance, if the criticism was that I had not made a hospital visit when, in fact, I had not known about the person's admission, I sympathized and said how important it was to me to have heard and to make the call. Underneath the person's anger might have been a fear of being neglected. Reassuring the person of my concern helped. If there was failure of a pastoral duty, then I apologized and promised to visit.

Clarify the complaint. I would begin by trying to sort out what was accurate and what was inaccurate information. By restating the complainant's words until they accurately reflected what the person was saying, we narrowed the com-

---

1. *The Book of Order: The Constitution of the Presbyterian Church (USA)* (Louisville: Office of the General Assembly, 2009), W-6.3009.

plaint down to something less general and more manageable. For instance, when someone thought I had said something in a sermon that was offensive, I tried to clarify what the person had heard and what I meant. With that clarification, often we were able to discuss the issue with less anger or defensiveness.

Work for resolution. I asked the person, "Where can we go from here?" Did the person insist on holding a grudge or want to work for resolution? If the person would not work for resolution, I suggested that we meet in the next week. If my apology was called for, then it was forthcoming. Most often, people were able to accept an apology and admit that we all make mistakes. Sometimes a person was not able to accept an apology, often because the person's view of the minister was unrealistic. However, in giving these simple examples, I do not mean to imply that dealing with criticisms is easy. Misinformation can turn into false accusations, and unattended hurt feelings can fester into grudges. There are times when pastors need to bring in a third party to help work for resolution.

There are other differences, such as those between committees, between member and board, or between member and member. Several strategies can be used depending on the situation. First, avoid being triangulated, that is, pulled into taking sides or being given the responsibility to solve another's problem. The pastor can also volunteer to help others negotiate their differences.

Second, encourage those with differences to try and resolve them rather than ignoring them until they harden, or refer them to some higher body. For instance, if church school teachers disagree about curriculum or use of space, help them wrestle with the problem. If it cannot be resolved at that level, then recommend that they ask the Christian education committee of the session to help. If those closest to the problem work on it, a more satisfactory solution might be reached, and the participants take responsibility for carrying it out.

Third, when working with groups, encourage them to describe the problem more than once, and from different perspectives. When does the problem occur? Does it happen after some other event? Does it happen when people are tired, or overburdened, or lacking clear directions, or when they have little input in the endeavor? Ask them to reframe the problem so that the most important impediment is clearly stated. Reframing the problem often leads to developing options for resolution.

Fourth, work for a consensus rather than a simple majority. This takes longer and requires patience, but in the long run it makes for more satisfactory solutions. To sustain a group's ability to work successfully, it is important to assure the participants that their considered judgments are as important as making decisions. However, when it becomes apparent that a clear difference of opinion prevents consensus, it is fair to rely on democratic procedure and let the majority rule. If the vote is close, and does not reflect the will of a substantial majority, it is wise to refer the problem for more study.

Handling conflict is different from resolving differences. Differences in opinion can be talked through. Conflicts often involve anger, resentment, and grievances. Conflicts in the church threaten the "peace, unity, and purity" of the church, and thus become the concern of the institution. Handling conflict often involves using the power of a governing body to keep both parties at the table, maintain order, subdue personal attacks, and insist that solutions can be found if both parties are willing to try. A solution may well have to be reached by a democratic vote, and the losing party might be angry at the result. However, the order of the institution and the freedom of the majority must be maintained.

Most denominations have a book of polity that lists measures for dealing with conflict, but before a situation requires judicial action, other steps can be taken.

At one time my congregation had a member whose professional responsibility was conflict resolution for various corporations. He did two things for us. He taught our leaders resolution skills, often using the book *Getting to Yes.*[2] And he volunteered to handle difficult conflicts either in the church or in community work where the church was engaged with other groups. In both instances he was a great help.

Differences in a church are not only inevitable, they are also often the pathway to improvement. It is better not to ignore them but to acknowledge to the concerned that, as a pastor, you know they are doing their best and offer your services as moderator. If we seek to listen and respond in all honesty, and if we can engage others in the peacemaking process, then even these stormy winds can be negotiated.

DISCUSSION QUESTIONS

1. *What are pastorally appropriate strategies for dealing with conflict within the congregation? What if the conflict is directed to the pastor?*

2. *How might conflict be used as an occasion for growth or improvement of the congregation?*

3. *To whom can pastors turn for help in resolving conflicts in the congregation?*

---

2. B. Fisher and W. Ury, *Getting to Yes: Negotiating Agreement without Giving In* (New York: Penguin, 1981).

CHAPTER THIRTEEN

Baptisms and Marriages

 A GRANDMOTHER ASKED her minister to baptize two grandchildren while they were spending a week with her when their parents were on vacation. The parents were not church members. One parent had been baptized and reared in the church, the other was not sure what she believed; and the grandmother, a devout Christian, wanted her grandchildren to receive the sacrament of baptism. It is possible that the children could have understood an explanation of baptism, but it was not certain that there would be familial follow-up in a church.

What is the right thing to do? Ordinarily, we view the sacrament of baptism as John Calvin did. He wrote that it is the "initiation by which we are received into the society of the church, in order that, engrafted in Christ, we may be reckoned among God's children."[1] In the baptism of infants, the parents promise to rear the children in the Christian faith.

---

1. John Calvin, *Institutes of the Christian Religion*, trans. Ford Lewis Battles (Philadelphia: Westminster, 1960), 4.15.1.

This involves becoming a part of the life of worship, learning, fellowship, and the mission of a congregation. Likewise, the congregation promises to "guide and nurture by word and deed with love and prayer, encouraging him/her to know and follow Christ and to be a faithful member of this church."[2] In this way it is hoped that the grace conferred and signified in baptism by God becomes real to the child. As the child worships God, apprehends God's love, learns about Jesus, and then partners with other fellow Christians in mutual support and in the mission of the church, the promise of God's grace signified by baptism becomes real in the life of the believer.

Parents who are not Christians or church members but want their children baptized are asked to meet with the pastor to learn what profession in Jesus Christ means. The pastor also explains what membership in the church offers. If the parents profess their faith in Jesus Christ and unite with the church, the sacrament can be administered to the child. Calvin stated clearly that baptism and faith and life in the church are all connected: "Accordingly, let those who embrace the promise that God's mercy is to be extended to our children deem it their duty to offer them to the church to be sealed by the symbol of mercy, and thereby arouse themselves to a sure confidence, because they see with their own eyes the covenant of the Lord engraved upon the bodies of their children."[3] By the commitment of parents in the life of the congregation and the nurturing of faith by the church, the promise of God's grace can become a living reality in the lives of the baptized. For children old enough to understand that baptism is the beginning of the

2. "The Sacrament of Baptism," in the *Book of Common Worship*, prepared by the Theology and Worship Ministry for the Presbyterian Church (USA) and the Cumberland Presbyterian Church (Louisville: Westminster John Knox, 1993), pp. 403-15.

3. Calvin, *Institutes*, 4.16.9.

Christian life, but who come without parental accompaniment and commitment, a member of the congregation could act in an educative and supportive role.

Can the sacrament have any efficacy if an infant is baptized without a family member who could oversee the infant's involvement in the church? Or is the sacrament a supernatural gift assuring the baptized of God's particular blessing? How is this different from magic or some sort of "divine insurance policy"? Calvin was careful to state that there is no magic power in the water: "not because such graces are bound and enclosed in the sacraments so as to be conferred upon us by its power, but only because the Lord by this token attests his will toward us, namely that he is pleased to lavish all these things upon us."[4]

In Calvin's view, the power of the sacrament is in the Word, meaning education in the evangelical love of Christ. Calvin was diligent in opposing "[a] magical conception of baptism in which the application of the water itself, apart from the norms conveyed in the proclamation of the gospel narrative and without faith, brought about salvation and eternal life with the triune God."[5]

In the case of the grandmother at the beginning of the chapter, I administered the sacrament of baptism to her grandchildren and asked her to bring their parents to meet with me when they returned from vacation. In that meeting, the grandmother explained her feelings for her grandchildren and her faith in God. I explained why I had administered the sacrament — saying that it was a sign of God's love for their children and that it was our hope that in the future the Spirit of God

---

4. Calvin, *Institutes*, 4.15.14.

5. Gordon S. Mikoski, *Baptism and Christian Identity* (Grand Rapids: Eerdmans, 2009), p. 155.

would lead the children to become acquainted with God's revelation of love in Jesus Christ. The parents were irritated by the license we had taken, but after extended conversation they understood the depth of her concern for her grandchildren and her deepest wish that they might possibly come to know the love of God in the future. They also understood that in some manner both of us believed in the strange working of God's Spirit and the possibility that this act was the beginning of a life in Christ.

Still, the question remains: Does administering the sacrament without a church to teach the Word of God's grace through the life, death, and resurrection of Jesus bestow divine grace? The grandmother and I acted in the hope that in some manner the Spirit would, through believers in the future, tell these children that they belonged to the covenant made in Christ. At the same time, this is an exception that should not become the usual practice.

Another situation requiring pastoral wisdom involves a request to perform the ceremony of marriage. "For Christians, marriage is a covenant through which a man and a woman are called to live out together before God their lives of discipleship."[6]

When couples who are not church members ask a minister to perform their marriage ceremony, how should the minister respond? In such situations, I meet several times with the couple to talk about their relationship, explain the meaning of Christian marriage, and explore the possibility of finding a church in which they would become active. Our meetings include not only conversation about their relationship, but also a review of the benefits of congregational life: worshiping to-

---

6. *The Book of Order: The Constitution of the Presbyterian Church (USA)* (Louisville: Office of the General Assembly, 2009), W-4.9001.

gether, meeting friends with similar values, learning the meaning and dynamic of forgiveness, receiving support in difficult times, and taking advantage of courses offered to the newly married and to new parents.

If one was a Christian and the other a member of another religious tradition, then we talked about their life of worship. Often, they compromised on a "neutral site" for future worship, or they agreed to worship in two congregations. I also asked them what they had talked about in terms of rearing children. In many cases, they avoided the question. I did not try to force a resolution but only introduced the subject. Again, I would describe the manner in which the church extends God's blessings through the worship, learning, service, and fellowship life of the congregation. After reflecting on such conversations, many joined either the Lawrenceville church or some other church. In time, they discovered that both acts – the sacrament of baptism and the ceremony of marriage – were, with the help of the church, the beginning of a new life that was rich in meaning and blessed with grace.

Some making these requests did not want to make the commitment to join a church. They believed that blessings from God came from the ceremony itself. In their opinion, when the minister refused to conduct the ceremony unless they promised to live within the worship and fellowship of a congregation, he was treating them unfairly. I reminded them that marriage is a civil contract between a woman and a man, and they did not need their service to be conducted by clergy to be married. There are, indeed, countries where most marriages are conducted by civil authorities, and later blessed in a church service.

At a dinner one evening, I posed these situations to three couples who were marginal members of churches. They thought I should accede to both requests without making any conditions. Baptism, to them, was an action by which God's blessing was conferred through the clergy upon the child, assuring the child of divine help. Neither should church membership be a condition for marriage. Their view was that marriage in a church also assures us of God's protection. I explained that Reformed tradition understands the congregational or church community as the time and place where we receive God's blessings. But the notion of the clergy possessing a blessing that can be conferred was important to them; and the understanding of participation in the congregation's worship and communal life as the source of blessing was hard to grasp.

DISCUSSION QUESTIONS

1. *How do you understand the meaning and efficacy of baptism?*

2. *What ecclesial requirements must parents meet to have their child baptized?*

3. *Under what circumstances might you refuse to perform a wedding?*

CHAPTER FOURTEEN

An Unexpected Renewal of Faith

EVEN WE MINISTERS are not immune to a diminishing faith and a loss of hope. The challenge is to revitalize our faith and renew our sense of hope. In my middle years as a pastor, my enthusiasm for pastoral work and preaching diminished. When I read the Gospels and the Epistles, I could not recover that sense I previously had of what the Scripture was conveying to our world. The gospel message seemed irrelevant for the salvation we need from the dangers around us.

Then, one day, a member brought a Pentecostal pastor from Haiti to my office, hoping that I would make a contribution to his work from my discretionary fund. I listened guardedly, wondering if he was just lining his own pockets. He worked in Port-au-Prince, in the poorest slum in the Western Hemisphere. He began his ministry in the streets, gathering children with stories of Jesus and then asking them to invite their parents to a local house on Sunday morning for services. From there, he went to an abandoned building, finally leading the congregation to buy a field that had been used as a trash dump. The congregation grew rapidly and soon built a large, rectangular, cinder block building for worship. Later, some adjoining classrooms were added for weekly adult classes and Sunday classes. He enlisted financial help from some small churches in Texas where he had gone to a Bible college. With that work under way, he called together two other congregations: one in the mountains and one in the sugar cane district. These were smaller and the people even poorer. I gave him a contribution because he did, in fact, seem sincere about bringing the gospel to the poor. He came back the next year, spoke of progress, and showed photographs. He kept using the words "the Lord led me" or "the Lord provided." He took no credit for himself, and while he appreciated what the people did, he was always certain that "it was the Lord's doing." His words, different from the religious language I knew, had the ring of both experience and truth. He invited me to go to Haiti, and I accepted.

When I got off the plane in Port-au-Prince, the air felt like a blast furnace, accompanied by smells of diesel fuel, burning garbage, concrete dust, and decay. Small children pulled at my clothing, begging for coins. Pastor Luc drove me to an old, decrepit French hotel, where I stayed. The next day we traveled into the mountains to the small church Pastor Luc had begun. We were surrounded by the villagers, mostly members of the church, and passed out bags of rice and beans. That night we were part of a worship service. The next day Pastor Luc explained that we would baptize the local voodoo shaman whom the local village people went to for blessings, curses, and cures. She had decided to become a Christian when her husband showed an interest in a woman of the local congregation. Pastor Luc had given her instructions. We climbed a rocky path to her hut to baptize her. She showed us a circle of ashes where she had burned her voodoo implements. In her one-room hut we stood in a circle, and she went to her knees.

An African American woman who had accompanied us, and who had memorized the Gospel of Mark, recited parts that had to do with the casting out of demons, and Pastor Luc interpreted. Then we put our hands on her head, and he asked me to offer a prayer committing her to God. We left her hut, had a celebratory lunch, and returned to Port-au-Prince. The next day we went to his small church in the sugar cane district. Small children with red hair and swollen bellies from malnutrition came slowly forward to welcome us, and again we handed out bags of rice and beans. We held a service; Pastor Luc talked to the congregation's lay leaders; and we returned to Port-au-Prince.

On Sunday, in Port-au-Prince, the congregation of a thousand gathered for worship. They came dressed in their colorful best, praised God, and called out to Jesus. I preached while Pastor Luc interpreted. Following worship, but still gathered in this large room, the people spoke of the change that the Christian faith had made. Now, they shared the little food they had, and bought funeral plots for each other. They taught their children French and English, and took classes in sewing and bicycle repair. Members also adopted children whose parents had died. There had been a reduction of drunkenness, wife beating, and fighting. Pastor Luc spoke constantly of depending on the leading of the Spirit.

My own faith was revitalized by what I had seen. Seeing the people of Haiti was like looking into the world of the Gospels. There was the same poverty, broken bodies, beggars, and the rich passing by. The faith of Pastor Luc and the congregations reminded me of the early churches described in the Acts of the Apostles. The power of preaching was evident as people listened intently and responded in song and prayer. Their life together as believers fought off the depredations of sin and suffering. I left Haiti with the hope that just as the power of the gospel was real there, so could it be real in Lawrenceville even though it was outwardly a different world.

When I returned to Lawrenceville, I preached sermons about Pastor Luc's ministry and the people who lived by prayer and faith. Several members decided also to travel to Haiti, taking with them local doctors, nurses, and bags of medications. Trips in alternate years became an important part of the church's mission program, and Pastor Luc visited us in the years we did not go to Haiti.

Seeing faith at work was evidence of the Spirit. As we related our experiences, others in the congregation stepped forward because they wanted to revitalize their faith and expand the purpose of their lives. Life in suburbia had seduced them into thinking hard work, success, and affluence would give meaning to their lives. When they came into contact with Pastor Luc, or went to Haiti, they were excited by the faith they saw, and sought the same power of faith. Thus were my faith and theirs revitalized by a man and his congregation that were part of a very different Christian tradition — one that recognized the work of the Spirit.

There are many ways of revitalizing one's faith. Jim McCloskey, who initiated Centurion Ministries — a ministry for clearing innocent prisoners who have been sentenced to death — has cleared more than forty innocent men and women. As he visits them he collects data that he, his associate, and volunteer lawyers use to prove innocence. When he tells his stories, he expresses his amazement at the faith of these incarcerated men and women, as well as their willingness to forgive those who conspired against them. Seeing their faith, he says, revitalizes his.

Christians around the world risk their health and safety in the cause of Christ. They feed the refugees of Africa, try to make peace between the warring factions of Palestine and Israel, work to end diseases bred by poverty in villages in South America, end the flow of children for purposes of prostitution, and gather into safe places the young people who wander the city streets at night. As they are involved in the task of saving others, they discover the power of faith and the fruits of compassion.

It is sometimes said, "Charity begins at home," but the issue is not charity. The issue is revitalizing our faith by participating in the work of God.

DISCUSSION QUESTIONS

1. What might be some of the signs of spiritual stagnation for a pastor?

2. How might one discern the call of God to engage in mission for a particular place (i.e., local, national, and international)?

3. How does your theology of the Holy Spirit relate to your personal renewal and the renewal of a congregation?

CHAPTER FIFTEEN

The Least of These

THE PSALMIST EXCLAIMED, singing about the temple:

> Even the sparrow finds a home,
>   and the swallow a nest for herself,
>   where she may lay her young,
> at your altars, O LORD of hosts,
>   my King and my God.
>
> (Ps. 84:3)

Jesus made the same point even more dramatically when telling a parable of the reception of the hungry, thirsty strangers, unclothed and sick, entering the kingdom of God on Judgment Day, "Truly I tell you, just as you did it to one of the least of these who are members of my family, you did it to me" (Matt. 25:40).

Within the congregation's comfort zone, members are often able to help one another. If a family is burned out of their house, church members rally around with housing and clothing, sometimes even helping them build a new house. But when the calamity is beyond the congregation's experience, the tendency is to look the other way, not from disinterest but from ignorance and discomfort.

Such was the case when Jim, a church member, was diagnosed as having a fatal skin cancer. His friends knew about his condition and were upset. He continued to come to worship on Sundays, but customary greetings by friends and acquaintances were forced, and asking about his future was awkward. As he became weaker, he found a chair and sat at one end of the church fellowship hall. As his friends became more distressed, fewer stopped by to speak. His condition worsened and he could no longer come to church; in a short time he died.

A few weeks later some of his friends talked about what they perceived as their failure to comfort Jim. They noted the irony that a Christian community, one that proclaims victory over death, could not find the words to say to Jim. Why were we not able to overcome our discomfort in spite of our friendship with Jim? they wondered.

Doesn't culture teach us not to speak to one another about personal matters, and what is more personal than our dying? And doesn't culture teach us not to embarrass another by referring to the person's troubles or weaknesses, or open our own hearts and express our own sorrows? How, then, can we express our love?

Can we learn the language of faith? Can we learn to say something like, "Jim, I am very sorry to hear about your troubles. I surely hope that the doctors can help. But I want you to know that I'm praying for you, for your faith and hope – I pray for the faith and hope of all of us." When a Christian community talks about faith and hope, it is showing its care for those it loves.

We did learn from our experience with Jim. Sometime later a determined mother forced the congregation to look at her son in a new light. Billy had a severe developmental disability and an IQ of probably a four-year-old even though he had just turned fourteen. His father had died, and his mother worked as a cashier in the dining center of a corporate headquarters. She brought Billy to church every Sunday, sometimes staying with him in the church school class, sometimes letting him sit with her in a pew. When Billy turned fourteen, she said it was time for him to join the confirmation class and become a member of the church.

Join the church! How could he do that? Our confirmands learned the books of the Bible and the meaning of the Apostles' Creed, and were asked to write their own confessions of faith to read before the session. In the class we taught them a brief history of the Christian church, the Reformation, and the basic beliefs of the Presbyterian Church. If Billy were in the class, he would not comprehend, and other children might laugh at him. But his mother persisted, so we included him in the regular class and met with him privately during the week. In the class, Billy smiled and enjoyed being with the others who, in fact, did not tease him. When the associate and I met with Billy at our special time, we told Gospel stories about Jesus: the lost sheep, Jesus and the children, Jesus' death and resurrection. We prayed with Billy, stressing that Jesus was our friend and explaining in prayer that we were talking to Jesus.

The night that the session met with the confirmands, we asked Billy who loved him, and he replied that his mother and Jesus did. He added that Jesus loved all children. We asked him what did Jesus want us to do and he answered, "Help people." We asked him why Jesus died, and he said bad people killed him. We asked him what happened after Jesus died, and he said Jesus was alive again. The session received Billy into membership. They said to him, "Billy, this is your church." And Billy responded, "This is my church."

When Billy became an adult, he went to live in a group

home in north Jersey. I did not see him again until twenty years later when he came back for his mother's funeral. I introduced myself to him, now a balding forty-year-old. He said, "This is my church."

At first it appears that the church did something for Billy, but actually his mother and Billy did a great deal for the church. His mother's faith and determination opened our eyes. Previously, we had assumed that one had to be "normal" to join the church. When Billy answered the session's questions, however, we heard the Spirit in Billy's answers. And when Billy responded to the session, "This is my church," we understood the ministry of the "least" among us. We remembered what a church really is: a gathering of the people Jesus calls, especially "the least of these." Members of the church were pleased that a way had been found to overcome admission into the church only for "normal" people. Members became thoughtful when they witnessed a confession that was so deeply sincere. Members were gratified that the church had found a way for inclusion by examining a person's heart.

Are we not all, at some point, among "the least"? Do not many of us have responsibility for "the least among us"? And will not a time of suffering come to all of us? It is reassuring to think that we shall be surrounded by friends who help us and who stay with us as we cross the waters. Recognizing the least, and acknowledging our kinship to them, is a sign of our love and gives relevance and vitality to the church.

Discussion Questions

1. *What key theological convictions are most relevant to thinking about and responding to people in the congregation who have disabilities or special needs?*

2. What requirements must a young person meet to be admitted into active, adult membership in the church?

3. What do persons with disabilities contribute to the life and mission of the church?

CHAPTER SIXTEEN

Two Guests in the House of the Lord

WE CHRISTIANS should be ashamed of what we have done, or allowed to have been done, at certain times in our history. We have exhibited terrible cruelty toward others, or at least a numbing disregard for the atrocities others have suffered. For centuries Christians either took civil rights away from Jews or persecuted them. The German Christian church made no attempt to stop the Nazi persecution of Jews while Christians in the United States largely ignored what was happening in Europe in the 1930s and 1940s.[1] There were Christians who were the exceptions, as the Jewish state has recognized with the Avenue of the Righteous. However, even in the United States, Jews were kept out of the mainstream of life until the pressure for equal civil rights prevailed, or their own excellent attainments became so influential that their place could not be denied.

My conviction is that Christian churches have an obliga-

---

1. Susannah Heschel, *The Aryan Jesus: Christian Theologians and the Bible in Nazi Germany* (Princeton: Princeton University Press, 2008).

tion to develop working relationships with the Jewish community, not only to prevent a continuation of victimization, but also to share the prophetic tradition of "seeking justice, doing mercy, and walking humbly" with the Lord God for the sake of the larger community. That conviction was shaped, in part, by my visit to a concentration camp in Germany. One summer after a semester at New College, I traveled through several countries in Europe. When in Germany, I went to Dachau and I walked down pathways between the wooden, gray dormitories. Thousands of emaciated Jews and Russian soldiers, taken prisoner, in their ragged, striped prison clothes lived in these buildings during World War II — working for the Nazis and waiting to die. A guide pointed out where prisoners had been hung or shot. Photographs pictured the bony, dead bodies, stacked like limbs from trees. We entered a crematorium where bodies had been burned. As I left, I felt a sense of shame that many Christians had either taken part in, or neglected to take actions against, this awful reality.

I remembered that walk when Mr. Kihn, a local Lawrenceville resident, asked if the church would house a group of liberal Jews who wanted to start Temple Micah. They chose that name because they felt strongly about the prophet's words:

[The Lord] shall judge between many peoples,
    and shall arbitrate between strong nations far away;
they shall beat their swords into plowshares,
    and their spears into pruning hooks;
nation shall not lift up sword against nation,
    neither shall they learn war any more.

(Mic. 4:3)

They would welcome all Jews who wanted to focus on a mission of peacemaking; furthermore, the organizers did not want to build their own building, as that would require high membership dues.

Here was an opportunity for the church to extend an act of hospitality in contrast to historic acts of persecution; allow both congregations to learn more about historic Jewish and Christian beliefs by inviting mutual participation in discussion groups and services of worship; and give witness in the larger community to the respect due to those who have often been ridiculed. Also, it was a chance to discover ways of relating to other faith traditions that might be useful in future dealings with such traditions as Islam.

When the request was presented to the session, some elders wondered if non-Christians could be allowed to worship in space that had been dedicated for Christian worship. However, without any written documentation from the dedication of the building in 1764, the elders decided that our worship of the God of Abraham, Isaac, and Jacob, the God who is father of Jesus Christ, was sufficient reason to approve the request.

I shared with the session my research of the apostle Paul regarding Jews. Paul's main disagreement with his fellow Jews was their requirement that observation of the Torah be the identifying sign of Judaism. For Paul, the identifying mark of belonging to God was faithfulness. Paul considered both Jews and Gentiles to be sinners: "Both Jews and Greeks . . . are under the power of sin" (Rom. 3:9b), but all have been saved by the grace of God. God's grace had been first revealed in the life of Abraham and then for Gentiles in the life, death, and resurrection of Jesus Christ (Rom. 5:1-11). Further, Paul believed that all Israel would be saved not when the Gentile Christians had converted Jews to Christianity, but when "the full number of the Gentiles has come in" (Rom. 11:25b). In *A Guest in the House of Israel*, Clark M. Williamson observes: "At the heart of the Jesus movement and the theology of Paul was a denunciation of every effort to place limits and conditions on the gracious love of God. That God justifies the ungodly, that this is true for all 'others' if it is true for Christians, that it is not their place to instruct God as to the limits to be put on the divine grace, that God can and will do new things that none of us can either imagine or anticipate — all this is at the heart of Christianity's apostolic witness."[2] Paul placed no limits on God's grace, and neither could the elders of the Lawrenceville church.

The Presbyterian General Assembly in 1987 took a supporting position. It stated that the church, being made up primarily of those who were once aliens and strangers to the covenants of promise made to Abraham, had been grafted into the people of God by the life and death and resurrection of Jesus the Messiah.[3]

The session took several steps to bring this plan about. First, it shared some of the history of persecution of Jews by Christians with the congregation. Second, it reviewed the relevant Scripture, hoping to balance some of Scripture's anti-Jewish statements. Third, it noted that these Jews were our neighbors. Fourth, it based the relationship on generosity, not a business arrangement. Over the years there has been no rental charge, and Temple Micah has been financially generous to the church on an annual basis and for capital fund building improvements.

Most members appreciated the events that featured interfaith dialogue and cooperation. Temple Micah used our community rooms on Friday nights and our meetinghouse on Yom Kippur and Rosh Hashanah. Members of the church staff read

2. Clark M. Williamson, *A Guest in the House of Israel* (Louisville: Westminster John Knox, 1993), p. 265.

3. "A Theological Understanding of the Relationship between Christians and Jews," GA Minutes (1987), 417-24.

from the Hebrew prayer book at these occasions. We held periodic Seder meals in the fellowship hall with both congregations attending. We also participated in the annual *Kristillnacht*[4] remembrance services at Rider University. One year the service was held at the church. When another Jewish temple, Adath Israel, constructed a new place of worship, vandals painted swastikas on the signs. A member of the Lawrenceville church cleaned up the signs, and others wrote letters of support for the temple to the newspaper. In the thirty-plus years of the Presbyterian Church of Lawrenceville–Temple Micah relationship, the response of the congregation has been favorable.

The session and general members with whom I spoke did not regard this relationship with a sense of condescension. I think most simply felt that it made sense for two religious groups who had a common history to use the same building. Of course, each group was aware of the differences. How could we not be when the Christian symbols were removed from the meetinghouse on the eve before Sabbath? But I did not hear words that expressed resentment, rather the awareness that even with common roots, we were different in important ways. Not every member approved of the session's decision, but enough did so that their decision prevailed.

It is possible that the manner by which this shared use of space and feelings of neighborliness were accomplished will serve as a model for future attempts at interfaith cooperation. It is a formidable challenge for churches to establish dialogue with people of the Islamic faith and, even more so, to encourage people of the Jewish, Christian, and Islamic faiths to make

4. *Kristillnacht* means "the Night of the Broken Glass" and refers to a night in 1938 in Germany when the Nazis destroyed Jewish homes and businesses. This marked the beginning of the Holocaust.

efforts to know each other better. However, such efforts will hopefully reveal ways we can build justice and peace together.

DISCUSSION QUESTIONS

1. *What is your theological understanding of the status of the Jewish community?*

2. *Under what conditions or circumstances would you agree to share the church's space with other religious groups?*

3. *Would your theological beliefs allow you to pray in public or in the presence of people from other religious traditions? Why or why not?*

CHAPTER SEVENTEEN

Meddling in Community Affairs

C HURCH MEMBERS can have varied responses to sermons that preach the biblical imperative to join the Spirit in "establishing God's just, peaceable, and loving rule in the world,"[1] or seek to lead the church in that mission. The responses are usually "You are meddling in politics," or the pastor is admonished, "Don't let the church become political."

Yet, when the biblical mandates are taken seriously, pastors and church members will encounter community situations that call out for justice and peace. Church members will discover families without food or homes, sections of town where the garbage is rarely collected, drug dealers on the street corners, and immigrants willing to work hard and honestly needing representation. How involved can a church become in helping people in distress without becoming "political"? If a church focuses on "establishing God's just, peaceable, and loving rule in the world," will it have traded the "spiritual" for the

---

1. *The Book of Order: The Constitution of the Presbyterian Church (USA)* (Louisville: Office of the General Assembly, 2009), W-7.4002.

"secular"? Questions like these required answers early in my pastorate in Lawrenceville.

When I first arrived in Lawrenceville in 1960, it never occurred to me that just a few miles to the south of this pleasant village was an isolated area of mainly African Americans called Eggerts Crossing. I discovered its existence at Christmas time two years later when I joined church members delivering turkeys to residents in the area. At one house, the elderly woman who lived there invited us in. Standing in her living room, we could look through the floor and see the ground. The cold air rushed in and there was no heater; and if there had been, it would not have overcome the cold. Her home was one among hundreds of decrepit buildings in the area. When questioned, the township housing officer answered that he did not condemn these houses because there was no other place for the residents to live.

I had met the pastor of the First Baptist Church of Eggerts Crossing at a clergy lunch, and we arranged for a joint meeting of the session with some of the Baptist church's leaders. Our guests, four African American men and two women who had lived in the area for many generations, described the area and the improvements they believed should be made. They wanted an Operation Head Start for preschool children, low-cost loans for home repair, free dental care, better relationships between blacks and whites in the township, and most of all, better housing. Soon after, other leaders of that community, organized by Fred Vereen, notified the session and church members of similar concerns. A determined coalition of church people and community members was developed. This group made formal application to the session for support both in personnel and finances.

The request raised two strategic issues involving pastoral leadership. First, because such involvement would be the first of its kind for the church, the issue would be potentially controversial and require sensitive handling. Specifically, we had to consider if the congregation was ready to perceive the biblical mandate regarding justice and mercy. Would church members understand a venture by the session established as a community effort, or would it be perceived as an inappropriate task for a church or an attempt to "politicize" the church? Had the preaching, education program, and history of the church's mission prepared the congregation for involvement in such a community effort?

The second issue had to do with management. If the pastor and session agreed that such a ministry was part of the church's mission, what was the role of the pastor as preacher and teacher? How should the pastor's advocacy be expressed in the life of the congregation and in the public eye? If a significant portion of the congregation hesitated to support the mission, did that influence the role of the pastor as mediator? How direct should the pastor and session be in countering rumors and false accusations that arose from either ignorance or opposition that was inspired by a desire to keep community power from being more broadly dispersed?

In the two years of my pastorate, much of my preaching had been from the prophets of the Old Testament, with their emphasis on justice and righteousness. Many New Testament texts focused on Jesus' concern for those who were without the resources of the rich. This laid the groundwork for the session's decision to support these community efforts. The session decided to become a partner in this community development effort, but did not use that terminology. It expressed only its desire to work with fellow Christians who were black and who lived nearby in deplorable conditions.

Having made this decision, the session began to involve members of the church. Some joined committees of African

Americans from the Eggerts area and from the Baptist church to start an Operation Head Start, a program for preschool children. Others solicited township residents for financial capital to begin a low-cost loan program so residents could repair their homes. Others bought food in wholesale amounts and sold the items at cost to the residents. The most controversial plan involved building housing units for low- and moderate-income families. The opinions of Lawrenceville church members were mixed; however, there was enough congregational support to mute that dissent. Also, because the session, not the congregation, governs a Presbyterian church, the session's decision prevailed.

Citizens of the township who had experience acquiring land and securing state funding joined Fred Vereen and his group from the Eggerts area. The work took several years and involved many bitter political struggles. But finally the land was purchased; approvals were secured, blueprints were made, and money was raised for construction. One citizen served gratis as an attorney. Two employees of the New Jersey state government had connections with the Johnson administration and made it possible for the project to receive federal funding. An architect donated his services. As the movement forged ahead, other churches became supportive.

The opposition was determined to stop the project and used delaying tactics in the township hearings. Those who opposed the effort claimed that these housing units would be occupied by the poor and lawless from Trenton — a neighboring city. Many feared an influx of African Americans from the nearby city of Trenton to the township — this fear reflecting the prevailing racism of the time.

After four years of overcoming political roadblocks, an attractive development for 100 families was constructed and filled with occupants. Celebrations were held to which hundreds came; at the most memorable one, many of the political opponents were seated on the dais as honored guests. When I questioned Fred Vereen about this, he replied, with a sly smile, "that they were friends now." That was a lesson worth remembering: one does not bear grudges, but works always to build coalitions.

The effort did not end with the opening of the housing. A few years later, Fred reported that the children of Eggerts Village were still part of a ghetto. Many of them had only a single, working, parent. Most did poorly in the township schools, and there was no one to lead them to township athletic programs. Many dropped out of school, and few were prepared for employment. The superintendent of schools promised tutoring help in the village, and the Lawrenceville church helped with funds and committee leadership. Now college graduates from the village are returning to help others.

Neither the elders nor I had any experience in community development. Reflecting on this experience, we recognized steps that served us well along the way. First, we had developed a theological reason for supporting the black Christians in the township. Some of those involved gave "being good neighbors" as the reason. However, in sermons and in forums held after worship, many said that Christians are called by Christ to help those who are victims of injustice, and others spoke of the "power and principalities." We viewed inadequate housing, limited schooling, and poor access to medical care as products of the forces against whom the Spirit strives. Our theological rationale challenged racism, with its disdain of blacks and its institutionalized injustices.

Second, the session and committees constantly sought church members to support the work. The work and the reasons for it were never hidden, but were publicized often in the life of the congregation. As church members joined the effort, we made their support known to all.

Third, I used sermons to give the theological basis for helping other Christians improve their community, but I refrained from making public statements that could be quoted in the newspapers. I did write or urge the session to write to the town council at different times calling attention to the needs of the Eggerts community. I explained the project to people in the congregation who were either opposed to or dubious about the session's effort. I tried to bring the doubters into contact with those doing the work so they could meet the people with whom we were linked in these efforts. With those in opposition, we never called approval of this mission a requisite for being a Christian. We attributed opposition to a lack of familiarity with blacks and suggested that they would discover that these folks shared the same values and hopes that we did.

Fourth, the session communicated to the congregation what steps were being taken to help mothers, children, and the aged in the Eggerts area. We wanted this understood not primarily as a political movement, but as a pastoral act by the church. However, some church members accused the church of "getting involved in politics" and dropped out of active membership or joined other churches.

Fifth, we invited community members and African American leaders from the Eggerts area to speak briefly in church describing the need for this community development, allaying fears, and praising the congregation for their support.

Sixth, we told the congregation what we learned about the "other," the African Americans who were our neighbors. We learned that both white and African American Christians shared many basic beliefs and behaviors. Both wanted their children to succeed in school and beyond; both wanted to live in safe communities and believed it was wrong in the sight of God for people to live in dreadful conditions; and both were willing to make sacrifices for the future of their children. Whites learned more about the origin of African American poverty. It was not from unwillingness to work, but from lack of education, training, and opportunity, and from the obstacles raised by racial prejudice. One claim made about America is that all you have to do is work hard to succeed, and we discovered that this was an oversimplification.

We learned that there were also differences. We whites were far more surprised by the political machinations of the opposition, such as not telling the truth and delaying council votes, than were the African Americans. The corporate or collective nature of sin had long been a part of their experience.

Finally, we learned that a determined minority could lead a community to do the right thing. This was a joint effort of people of faith. It was a ministry of laity that included people outside traditional religious groupings. There is a term in Jewish literature that describes who was involved. It was an effort by the "righteous" — by those who believed in trying to help the poor, who were benevolent, good of heart, and generous toward the needy.[2]

DISCUSSION QUESTIONS

1. *How might you go about mobilizing a congregation to respond to pressing human needs in the community in which the congregation is located?*

2. *What are some of the most formidable challenges that the congregation must face in developing partnerships in the local community?*

2. "Righteousness," in *The Interpreter's Dictionary of the Bible* (Nashville and New York: Abingdon, 1962), 4:85.

3. *Can you name three specific strategies that might lead to genuine partnership with groups or individuals from the community? Can you name three specific strategies that might inadvertently lead to a sense of paternalism?*

CHAPTER EIGHTEEN

Helping Laity Find Their Gifts

"**P**ASTOR, WE NEED more teachers." This is a typical cry. A persistent problem is finding church members to carry out the ministries and the mission of the church. Staffing the church school, filling the stewardship committee and other church boards, finding people to paint the kitchen — these are tasks that too often land on the pastor's desk. So, the pastor sighs and picks up the telephone.

But there is another way. It begins with the pastor changing certain assumptions, and then making these changes known to others. The first change is the assumption that the pastor's responsibility is to find people to do the work. The key is the word "work." Rather than the pastor asking people to take on the work of the church, it is the whole congregation's responsibility to help people identify their gifts. Paul writes about gifts: "Now there are varieties of gifts, but the same Spirit; and there are varieties of services, but the same Lord; and there are varieties of activities, but it is the same God who activates all of them in everyone. To each is given the manifestation of the Spirit for the common good" (1 Cor.

12:4-7). With the realization that the Spirit has given the gifts of Christ, it is clear that we are not trying to sign members up to do the work of the church. We are asking people to consider what gifts the Spirit has given them to use in the mission of the church as well as in their public or secular lives.

Hearts and minds were opened for the coming of the Spirit when a woman of the congregation spoke before hundreds of church women's groups. She had three questions for the audience: First, how many felt the word "power" described them? Very few raised their hands. Second, how many felt the word "leader" described them? Again, very few raised their hands. And third, how many knew of needs in their communities they wanted to meet? Almost everyone raised a hand. The speaker then told stories of women who had power when they banded together; who became leaders; and who met tough challenges in their neighborhoods. The speaker opened the way for the Spirit.

The pastor can also become acquainted with the congregation by discerning gifts. In the normal course of visitation, ministers become acquainted with congregational family members, where they live, and what work they do. However, as one on the lookout for the gifts of the people, the pastor seeks to know the members of the church "spiritually."

What does "spiritually" mean? Does it mean that such gifts are otherworldly? Interpreting Paul's words about gifts, the New Testament scholar Hans Conzelmann observed: "The essential point is precisely that everyday acts of service are now on a par with the recognized, supernatural phenomenon of the Spirit. Thus Paul is no longer oriented to the phenomenon, but to the community as the goal of the Spirit's working. He is showing the believer who has no ecstatic gifts that he is assigned 'his part,' and how he is assigned it. For the believer in question, grace is hereby made the key to his understanding of himself and his attitude toward his brothers."[1]

So it would be a mistake to think of gifts in a "spiritual" way if by that we mean they are not used in the ordinary duties of living. Pastors may look for a modern equivalent of "the utterance of wisdom," "working of miracles," "prophecy," and "discernment of spirits" (1 Cor. 1:4ff.). Does this person see possibilities for those who gather in trust and hope? Is this person able to discern in others a good heart and a willing spirit? Men and women who find their secular work too impersonal might sense that they have a gift for working with the young. A person who trains apprentices in a trade might discover he has a gift for working with those who are dyslexic or have attention-deficit problems. Pastors can use "their senses" to locate and discern those who will want to take on the acts of ministry.

The second assumption that needs changing is that a church activity or group has constantly to be kept on life support. There was a time when the Women's Association was very popular at Lawrenceville, and volunteers willingly came forward to serve as officers and circle leaders. In time, however, women were elected to the boards of the church. They also became part of the labor force and took jobs outside of the home. We had difficulty finding women to fill the spots, so the women concluded that a Women's Association was no longer needed. There were still small groups or circles for those who wanted them, but there was no longer any need for a large organization with dozens of slots to fill. If we had insisted that the association continue even though it was not needed, we would have turned gifts into duties and obligations — a burden laid upon people by tradition. Those who wanted to continue

---

1. Hans Conzelmann, *A Commentary on the First Epistle to the Corinthians* (Philadelphia: Fortress, 1981), p. 208.

to meet as a women's fellowship did so, often gathering to study books or stitch garments for homeless children.

However, some ministries are important, and yet pastors might have trouble finding the gifted. We can dig deeper for the meaning of the tasks. For example, has the congregation learned the meaning of the baptismal vows? How visible are the young to the rest of the congregation? Is adult education emphasized so that there is a developing crop of teachers? Can grandparents be involved with the young? What is at stake in terms of Christian identity for all of us in a world increasingly swayed by the values of entertainment?

The third assumption has to do with the pastor's view of authority. Inviting the laity into ministry also means taking their opinions and ideas seriously. Some pastors might be afraid this will lead to a challenge of their authority in the church, but pastors' authority is not to tell others what to do. It is to make it more likely that the Spirit can work through pastors in the church. While we pastors are responsible with the session for directing the mission of the church, we are not the sole leaders. It is not only our privilege but also our authority that leads us to say to others, "I believe you have gifts in this area." Helping members discover spiritual gifts fulfills one of the duties of the pastor.

To sum up, we are called to help laity find their ministry. A pastoral experience taught me this lesson. The congregation needed more pastoral care than the pastor could provide, so I met with the deacons, knowing that their tasks had been confined to putting on church suppers and doing the Sunday ushering. I reviewed the description of the work of the Board of Deacons in the *Book of Order*, and then suggested to them that they be directed by the church to provide pastoral care to the congregation. To that end, the pastoral staff assigned them to districts of members; the deacons were to make visits and report to the pastor any needs for attention. They agreed to do this. For the first two or three years, the deacons carried out this assignment faithfully, with probably 75 to 80 percent of the visitations being made. Gradually the visitations fell off while the officers unsuccessfully urged the deacons to make telephone calls, if not visits. The morale of the board suffered as deacons admitted they were not making contact with the members.

The president of the board said that most deacons felt inadequate in spite of the training offered, and they did not feel equipped to make pastoral calls. Suddenly, the light dawned! We had started at the wrong end — telling people what they should do instead of finding people with appropriate gifts. Now, we invited people forward who perceived that they had a gift for caring for people. Members were located who wanted to visit those in hospitals or help the homebound with their shopping, or who enjoyed visiting the elderly. In three years, the board was carrying out this pastoral ministry with enthusiasm. It came about because we assisted the laity in discerning and using their gifts.

By trial and error we developed a new way of beginning new missions. This involved setting forth the goal and calling for people who perceived that they had appropriate gifts to come forward and help us shape the mission from the beginning. We stumbled into a new way of beginning new missions and involving members of the church. The staff and officers were now the seekers of those with gifts, challenging the heart and soul instead of laying duties on reluctant shoulders. Willing workers now discovered their talents, and board conversations included Bible study and talk about faith and action.

As the news spread that membership meant an opportunity to add meaning to one's life, the need for the pastor to find volunteers diminished and the pastor's role became the more delightful task of offering opportunities for people to dig more deeply into their faith and find their ministries.

DISCUSSION QUESTIONS

1. *What is the minister's role in discerning, celebrating, and using the spiritual gifts of members of the congregation?*

2. *Can you identify four or five spiritual gifts that are not listed by the apostle Paul in his various enumerations of gifts?*

3. *By what processes might spiritual gifts be matched with particular ministries of the church?*

4. *How might the church assist its members in using spiritual gifts in vocational settings?*

CHAPTER NINETEEN

Developing Spirituality in the Governing Board

A T A RETREAT for pastors, one said, "I wish my session was more spiritual." When asked what he meant by "spiritual," he said he wished the leaders were more aware of the presence of God and Christ as they made their leadership decisions. Furthermore, he said that the session meetings were too much like the business meetings he had attended before he had gone to seminary. Elders coming to the meeting were worn from a day of work, hard travel, and the demands of family life. When the session meeting concerned only a budget deficit, a new curriculum for the church school, or a conflict between two groups, there was little about the evening that was spiritually and emotionally reviving.

Another pastor agreed, saying he wished his whole congregation were more spiritual. When this group of pastors explored the topic, they decided a spiritual life entailed a feeling of the presence of the holy, or as some described it, a sense that Jesus was near. Others in the group said being spiritual resulted from setting aside time to meditate and contemplate the blessings of God, leaving a person feeling serene or empowered, as if the Holy Spirit had descended upon the person.

On reflection, I have two reactions to this understanding of spirituality. First, spirituality means being faithful to God in our daily lives. Spirituality is not a state of mind in which God takes us away from concrete relationships, responsibilities, and problems, as if being spiritual meant we were above the realities of life. Neither is it a mood, an emotion, as if we were lifted up in ecstasy. Spirituality is like the faithfulness of Simeon and Anna (Luke 2:25-38), who came to the temple and lived on the temple grounds waiting for a sign from God that the Messiah had come. The sign was not thunder and lightning, nor a powerful prophet, but a humble family with its child. Both of these aged people, by virtue of their piety, or faithfulness, recognized the Messiah and praised God. Spirituality means being faithful on a daily basis. A colleague likens it to marriage; marriages are held together by mutual faithfulness to the vows, not by high moments, nor are they torn apart by low moments. We live in faithfulness; that is akin to living a spiritual life.

My second reaction is that being spiritual is about how we live our lives each day, even doing the most mundane of tasks. For instance, a session was once "cleaning the rolls of the church," meaning they were removing from the membership rolls the names of members who had not been active in the life of the congregation. Being active meant attending worship and/or supporting the church financially. This had financial repercussions, as the local church had to pay the national body a certain sum for each member to cover certain administrative costs. The session was obliged to contact those who did not attend or support and encourage them to become active again. However, this particular session had not cleaned the rolls in several years, and the task of contacting inactive members seemed daunting. Most of the members of the session agreed that they should ignore this duty, as they thought they would not be able to reactivate the members. But they did agree that it was a sound business decision to make for the financial well-being of the church. Then one officer spoke up, saying, "What is our spiritual responsibility for these brothers and sisters in Christ?" Spirituality is more about how we carry out our tasks, how we treat others, what are our priorities and values, than it is about achieving a gnostic feeling of closeness to the Lord.

At Lawrenceville, we recognized we were succumbing to a business orientation in session meetings, so we started each meeting with forty-five minutes of prayer and continuing education. We prayed for members of the church. Our education focused both on content (Bible study, becoming more familiar with Presbyterian principles) and on spiritual growth. Learning to pray for each other, the congregation, the church at large, and the world was a part of our continuing study. We also discovered that the practice of *lectio divina* encouraged discussion of faith and the Bible. The *Directory for Worship*, especially chapters describing worship, prayer, witness, and the sacraments, was an important component of our study. We used theological texts, such as those written by Shirley Guthrie discussing Christian beliefs,[1] and those written by Douglas John Hall examining a theological understanding of suffering.[2] We were also intent on praying for members of the church and for the world in its suffering. Occasionally, a member would speak of a problem at work or in the home that our theological reading framed in a new way. The group was able to explore the

1. Shirley C. Guthrie, *Christian Doctrine*, rev. ed. (Louisville: Westminster John Knox, 1994).

2. Douglas John Hall, *God and Human Suffering: An Exercise in the Theology of the Cross* (Minneapolis: Augsburg, 1986).

various ramifications of trying to be faithful. I am convinced that our educational effort gave us the theological tools to think and speak in ways that freed us from some difficult dilemmas. It also became far easier to deal with the problems of personnel, policy, and program. As we came to know each other better, we built our sense of community and facilitated discussions of controversial subjects without rancor. By the time the meetings ended, the elders felt a sense of accomplishment and had renewed their sense of belonging to God.

Our method of developing spirituality did not focus on trying to "feel" the presence of God. Nor did we equate faith with emotional display. Of course, there is an emotional component to our lives as Christians. We do feel joy and gratitude. We do feel afraid or lonely. And there are moments when we are touched by a feeling that God loves us. But in the Reformed tradition, our faithfulness is not drawn from feelings or from "capturing" God in a private moment. The Reformed faith emphasizes that we are called to live faithfully, following the Lordship of Jesus Christ, the head of the church.

DISCUSSION QUESTIONS

1. *What are the key differences between a church governing board and a board of directors for a business or a nonprofit corporation?*

2. *How would you define the term "spirituality," and what does it mean to you? To lay leaders? To members of the congregation?*

3. *What would be the key elements of your pedagogical strategy to develop the spirituality of the governing body of a congregation?*

CHAPTER TWENTY

Staff Dynamics

M ANY CHURCHES have a staff, and a having a staff means
having both opportunities and problems. A small
church might have a pastor, a part-time secretary, a part-time
custodian, someone responsible for the ministry of music, and
perhaps someone helping with Christian education. Other
than the pastor, these staff members might be volunteers or
paid a minimal amount. A large church might have a staff of
thirty or more (including those responsible for maintenance),
with various personnel representing specialized ministries.
The styles of staff leadership will vary – the smaller church
perhaps being more collegial, and the larger church being
more departmentalized with a more formal chain of command and reporting procedure.

We might expect church staffs to be models of collegiality
simply because they represent a Christian enterprise. But staff
dynamics are a complicated subject. Church staffs, like those
in the business and academic worlds, can be rent with jealousies, misunderstandings, resentments, bullying, and vicious
behavior.

It would be helpful if the leader and members of a church staff would base their behavior on Paul's understanding of divided communities. In a discussion of the centrality of the cross in Paul's theology, Theodore W. Jennings Jr. writes of the divided communities Paul addressed in his letters. Jennings states that Paul's chief concern in referring to the cross is "[n]ot a Christology but ecclesiology, not doctrine but the life of the community." Paul indicates his reason for writing: "I appeal to you . . . that all of you be in agreement and that there be no divisions among you" (1 Cor. 1:10).[1] Paul is referring to a report he heard about quarrels, bickering, and contention among the church members. Paul's ecclesiology is based on his understanding of the crucifixion of Jesus as an act of solidarity and good will on the part of God, an act that challenges and overthrows the power and prestige of the Roman Empire. Using this victory of love overpowers the secular humanism that dominates humanity and subjects people to slavery of all types. Paul declares that churches are also captive to powers like jealousy, fractiousness, discord, and divisiveness. But the power of the cross, which in its weakness is stronger than either the powers of Rome or the powers of divisiveness, can unify the churches in a spirit of solidarity and good will.

Staff dynamics was not a subject of study in seminary. As a recent graduate from seminary, I had little knowledge of the work of a pastor or the mission of the church. Fortunately, the senior minister was generous with his time, and I learned from the tasks given to me, from the staff meetings, and from regular informal meetings with the head of staff. My specific assignments included oversight of the deacons, the evangelism committee, and the young adults. I made many house

---

1. Theodore W. Jennings Jr., *Transforming Atonement: A Political Theology of the Cross* (Minneapolis: Fortress, 2009), p. 157.

calls on potential new members and shared the hospital calling with the staff. When the senior pastor was on vacation, I conducted funeral services and services of marriage. However, being an associate reduces the consequences of making mistakes. Everyone knew that the senior pastor was on hand to correct the staff's more drastic mistakes. He was willing to share his time and thought; in no way was he competitive or threatened by members of the staff. He did not play favorites, and never sought praise or reward for himself. He set a style not unlike the style Paul describes for the early Christian churches.

When I came to the Lawrenceville church, the staff was small. I was a solo pastor, with a part-time secretary, custodian, organist, and choir director. A seminary student was hired to help with the youth groups. In time the church membership grew to the high 800s. I became the head of a staff that consisted of one other person in a pastoral role, a part-time minister of music, a part-time organist, three or more seminary interns, a secretary, a business administrator, part-time secretaries, and a custodian.

I tried to copy the leadership style I had observed in my experience as an associate pastor. As the staff grew, each member of the staff worked within the boundaries of his or her work, and yet shared more general insights and opinions with the rest of the staff. The insights and opinions of secretaries had as much value as anyone else on the staff. Musicians, for instance, thought about Christian education, and the business administrator thought about our pastoral work. We sought to break down bureaucratic barriers, eliminate jealousies, and honor each person.

In my experience, the most difficult task in forming a staff is selecting the right people for the various positions. Difficulties happen at both ends. It is difficult for the person considering employment to know the culture of the particular church. What is the prevailing theology of the congregation and the head of staff? Does the head of staff want to be involved in every ministerial task, to the point of looking over the shoulders of colleagues? How is piety expressed? Is the chain of command more or less formal? How is success measured? Will the head of staff consider the associate more as a copastor or as one who works in a clearly defined area? It is not likely that we can find answers to these questions until we have worked together. If we can be adaptable, we can work out misunderstandings and potential conflicts along the way.

Likewise, the head of staff will have questions. It is difficult to know an applicant's character, personality, and work ethic. Is the associate a hard worker? Will the associate communicate with the congregation, understand the congregation's language, and challenge social mores that harm people without alienating the congregation? What sort of theology does the associate operate with? Does the associate have emotional needs with damaging consequences? Will the associate expect to share the pastor's role — to moderate the session and preach regularly? Answers will be forthcoming from the experience of working together. But again, we can adapt and flexibly deal with difficulties.

We had considerable success in choosing people from the congregation for paid staff positions and training or educating them for the work. A church member who was first a deacon and then president of the deacons' board showed great sympathy and good sense in helping church members with problems of life and death. She enrolled in appropriate courses at Princeton Theological Seminary and also received a degree in counseling at the College of New Jersey, all while employed as an associate for pastoral care. The church secretary showed talent and interest in administration and the care of the church buildings, and did a superb job as business administrator. As the church school program developed, a need emerged for a leader of the children's ministry, and the session selected a church member who, with special training, was a dynamo in helping young families take advantage of the church's ministry with children.

One downside of hiring congregational members is that feelings might be hurt when it is necessary to terminate employment. But my experience is that this happens less often than having to dismiss an employee whose background we had not known before hiring.

Heads of staff of churches overseeing thousands of members will give a different account of their role regarding the benefits and difficulties involved in having large staffs. There is no question in my mind that a staff, large or small, is a vital necessity for enlivening the ministry and mission of a church.

Discussion Questions

1. *Name three major challenges associated with being a member of a church staff.*

2. *What primary responsibilities does a head of staff have in leading and supporting the staff of a church?*

3. *How should the pastor relate to the personnel committee? To a search committee for a new staff member?*

4. *What primary responsibilities does an associate or assistant pastor have in functioning as a healthy member of a staff?*

CHAPTER TWENTY-ONE

Setting a New Course

W E DO NOT ordinarily think of Jesus as planning his mission. Yet, a case can be made that the story of his temptations (Matt. 4:1-11) is about decisions that defined his messiahship, and these decisions laid the groundwork for the planning of his mission. Following those decisions, his mission planning is reported in his first sermon in his hometown. It is

> to bring good news to the poor . . .
> to proclaim release to the captives
>> and recovery of sight to the blind,
>>> to let the oppressed go free,
> to proclaim the year of the Lord's favor.
>
> (Luke 4:18-19)

We can run out of ideas for the church's mission and feel as if the church is drifting into a downward slide. Meetings of the governing board leave church leaders bored. As pastors, we sometimes ask ourselves: Are we failures when our preaching does not light the fires of discipleship? Are we reduced to searching for the latest book that will suggest new missions for the church? When changes are needed in building space and use, church school curriculum, the service of worship, the role of the board of deacons, the music in worship, or pastoral calling, congregations begin to ask, "Why don't we do something about this?" Planning is helped when there is shared dissatisfaction with things as they are. A friend wisely said, "Needed change is based on wanted change."

How do we plan our mission? We are called to plan and work together to carry out the mission of the church. Pastors and members serve "mutually under the mandate of Christ who is the chief minister of all."[1] One method of doing this is to use a church planning process. Through this process new challenges are discovered, new people come forth, worn-out ministries are ended, new resources are found, and leaders once again are enthusiastic. It is helpful for leaders to periodically reexamine who they are and what they are doing.

The planning process used at the Lawrenceville church was constructed to inspire the leaders and congregation, and to revive the sense of mission.

The planning process began with the session. The first step was to clarify the session's responsibilities as the governing body. When its responsibilities had been reviewed, the session members reviewed how each responsibility was carried out and noted any problems. The planning process used was taken from *Effective Leadership for Today's Church* by Arthur Merrihew Adams. He pictured a planning wheel to describe the steps of the process, moving through the process as around the face of a clock. The steps are as follows: Purpose, Prospect, Prob-

---

1. *The Book of Order: The Constitution of the Presbyterian Church (USA)* (Louisville: Office of the General Assembly, 2009), G-6.0101.

lems, Possibilities, Projects, and Patterns.[2] The process itself began when officers met on Saturday mornings. At certain times, members were also invited to take part. We drew a large circle on a piece of paper. "Purpose" was written at the top position. Several hours were given to forming a statement of the church's purpose; biblical passages, the confessional documents of the church, and previous vision statements for guidance were used in thinking this question through.

When the participants were satisfied with "Purpose," they moved to the next task, reviewing the "Prospect," or the "outlook" and "landscape" of the church's situation. The word "Prospect" is used in the sense of an overview, as if we were standing on a hill and looking at what was below. In this section all the data known about community and church were written down. We came to know our congregation better than ever before, discovering what the age groups were and where members lived, worked, shopped, and entertained themselves. The staff asked questions that the group researched involving the population, local industry, recreation, places of poverty, schools, playgrounds, and patterns of commuting. Staff and members talked to welfare officers, police and fire company officers, teachers, township council members, and real estate agents. Our field of mission was better understood. To examine the larger mission of the church, the staff put church members in touch with the denomination's administrators for fraternal work in several parts of the world. Once these steps had been taken, the process moved along quickly and task forces were created to ponder new patterns of mission.

Continuing in a clockwise direction, the topic "Problems" was written at the next position. By comparing our purpose as

2. Arthur Merrihew Adams, *Effective Leadership for Today's Church* (Philadelphia: Westminster, 1978), pp. 115-16.

a church and the prospects, the situation in which we live, we were able to discern our problems.[3] After identifying problems, "Possibilities" was put in the next position. Here, we listed as many ways as we could think of for dealing with each problem. Such possibilities included doing a neighborhood house-to-house calling program, changing the hour of worship, making sure the nursery was handled competently, holding breakfasts on Sunday mornings for young families, and beginning a second service in an alternative mode.

Nearing the top position, "Projects" to be adopted were selected from the possibilities list. Finally, at the eleven o'clock position, the word "Patterns" was written. This had to do with the specific plans for each project, including leadership, space, timing, and finances that would be needed. Completing the circle, a comparison of results was made with the original purpose, to see if we were satisfied with our description of purpose.

At each step the congregation was invited to join a post-worship meeting on Sundays, and asked for their responses and suggestions. They pondered the church's purpose and contributed their own perspective. The meeting also gave them the opportunity to add their knowledge of the needs of the congregation and the township. As possible ministries were considered, volunteers indicated their interest.

This took several weeks. At Sunday meetings after worship, the officers restated our mission purpose until most people understood and agreed. We also shared our educational resources, using the Bible, the *Book of Confessions*, and the *Book of Order of the Presbyterian Church (USA)*. As people expressed

---

3. A simple example of problems: if one of our purposes was to worship God, and if there were very few thirty- and forty-year-olds in worship (assuming that they did live in the community), then our problem was that they were not being reached to worship God.

interest in various projects, we listed these people as future leaders.

Often participants wanted to move quickly past purposes and prospects to deal with projects, yet shortcutting the process was resisted. Establishing purposes provides an opportunity to study "The Church and Its Mission" in the PCUSA *Form of Government*. Putting this description into the words of participants gave everyone a new understanding of the church, one that would influence their understanding of mission.

The last conference of the planning event ended with worship on Sunday afternoon. The leaders met again the following Saturday. In the process of debriefing, the leaders declared that the planning sessions had been fruitful. They provided time for pruning ineffective and outworn ministries, and involved members in new and innovative ministries. The staff was not left with more to do because more members became active in the church's ministry and mission.

As the leaders reviewed the results, they noted ways that this was unlike corporate planning. These plans were not passed down from "on high." Whereas many other organizations are driven by goals that are set by management, the nature of the church as "the people of God" calls for goals to be set by the congregation and its representatives. The congregation takes its marching orders from the gospel and its ecclesiastical tradition. Thus, the method of planning not only involves the officers and leaders, but also gives opportunity to all church members as "the people of God" to engage in planning.

Second, leaders compared the results of the planning session with the purpose of a church in the Presbyterian tradition as described in "The Great Ends of the Church" section of the *Book of Order*.[4] As the people of God, we are called to proclaim

4. *The Book of Order*, G-1.0200.

the gospel, nurture the spiritual fellowship of the congregation, maintain worship, promote social righteousness, and exhibit the kingdom of heaven to the world. The leaders used this as a measuring rod and found that their results touched on each of these ministries.

Third, the leaders noted that churches are called upon to preserve tradition even as they discover new ways of working with the Spirit. Preserving tradition is important because we need to keep alive what is true and good. But if churches are not aware of the changing language of people, their changing schedules, and their struggles, they become irrelevant.

Another sort of planning is short-term planning. This happened once when the session wanted to provide a healthy environment for the youth of the community. A youth leader suggested holding dances for hundreds of young people. Once approval had been given, a task force proceeded to develop a "pattern" for the dances. On a piece of newsprint, the planning committee listed, hour by hour, the pertinent events and possible problems. Expectations and actions were listed (i.e., at 7:00 P.M. the band would arrive, the refreshments would be on the tables, and the youth would begin to arrive). In a column next to those expectations, unintended negative consequences were listed (i.e., the band would fail to show up, the refreshments would not be delivered, there would be fights among youth in the parking lot). Adjacent to these consequences, responses were listed for each possibility (have taped music ready, go to a store that sold refreshments, hire off-duty police officers to patrol the parking lot). Every hour was accounted for, including time until the parking lot was empty. Only a certain number of youth could enter (according to the fire code). Provision for supervision in the restrooms and for chaperones to wander around the room was made. Off-duty police officers were available in case there was trouble. Money received for admission was securely held. The church's no-smoking policy was to be observed; roving chaperones looked for drug use or potential fights. As a result of this careful planning, the parents in our congregation were willing to participate. Yet, in spite of all this planning, the dances lasted for only two years. An influx of young people from other towns led to violence at levels that could not be controlled.

Some members were critical of this ministry. At a session meeting, one elder asked why the church should make such a large effort for young people who were not part of the church. Another elder asked for a Bible and read the parable of the lost sheep. He noted that Jesus told this parable in response to a comment by the Pharisees and scribes, "This fellow welcomes sinners and eats with them" (Luke 15:2). Youth in Lawrence Township, as in many other areas, did not have a place to gather that was both fun and safe. The township had not supplied such a place. The elders believed that the church should make this effort.

The dances were held once a month for two years, but the church had to stop holding them after several fights occurred. In debriefing the whole project, the planners learned that a more regular monitoring of the event was important. At the same time, racial feelings were so heightened that it is not likely that our effort with young people, most of whom were not part of the church or the immediate community, would have succeeded – regardless of stricter monitoring.

When we leaders debriefed this program, we asked ourselves if this effort had been a failure. Some of the congregation considered it so since these dances had to be discontinued after two years, but the leaders did not agree. We considered it a worthwhile and successful effort. Seeing the need, putting together elaborate plans, and carrying them out to the best of our ability were reasons to call this a success. It was more important to try and then to call it off after two years, than to have ignored the problem. Also, the response of our own young people — as they saw us make an effort on their behalf — convinced them that the church was there for them.

Planning keeps an organization fresh since it continually uncovers new directions. At the same time, it offers opportunities for discontinuing practices that have outlived their usefulness. In summary, planning develops new missions, enlists more members in the church's ministry, and makes it possible for members to experience a renewal of faith and hope.

When the leaders of the Lawrenceville church engaged in planning sessions, they began the meetings with Bible study and prayer. The study and prayer focused on our faith in the Holy Spirit. In particular, we devoted our attention to the Acts of the Apostles and read those accounts with the assumption that the Holy Spirit was leading the apostles and the early church. As we planned, that helped us to look for signs that the Spirit was speaking to us through both the participants of the planning sessions and the events of the community that cried out for pastoral and evangelical attention.

Thoughtful discipleship calls for faithfulness to the mission of Christ's church combined with knowledge of the world into which the Spirit sends us. Discipleship calls for planning, knowing who we are, where we are, what the Spirit calls us to do and be, and what gifts have been given to us for our ministry.

DISCUSSION QUESTIONS

1. *What might serve as a theological rationale for engaging in a process of strategic planning in the congregation?*

2. *How should congregations use secular planning resources and models? Are there significant theological or ecclesial concerns*

that have to be taken into account when appropriating or using such models?

3. *What questions have to be asked to assess a strategic plan in the light of the gospel and the context of the congregation?*

The Surprising Presence

ONE EVENING I met with a group of retired pastors for dinner and conversations. After catching up with each other, we shared stories from our life in the church. At first we told stories of odd and humorous moments in ministry. One pastor told of a best man who passed out during a wedding from having had too much to drink the night before, and fell across the feet of the groom. He lay there until the benediction was pronounced. Another pastor told of having to jump into a grave before a graveside service to shovel out the dirt that had caved in during a torrential downpour, because the grave-digger was not present.

Then the stories turned. We told stories of a "surprising presence" in our ministries. This surprising presence was like what the disciples experienced as they strained at the oars. A presence came across the waves and met them in the midst of storm and struggle. Then the presence spoke: it was Jesus saying, "It is I; do not be afraid" (Mark 6:50). His presence restored the disciples, and they were able to row the boat to the far shore.

His surprising presence was the subject of many of our stories. There were times in our ministries when we were discouraged, fearing that we would fail because of exhaustion or strength of opposition to what we were trying to do. He came into our midst, most often through someone of faith and hope. That evening we told stories of the people of our congregations and of the surprising presence who had empowered us.

There was the immigrant family whom the church sponsored. The husband and oldest daughter returned many times to help their village. Their reports to our congregation brought a surprising presence, and we raised funds for a medical clinic and a new well for drinking water.

There was a young college graduate who grew up in the church and committed herself to the ministry of Jesus, working to free young girls and boys who were migrant workers on farms, and used for prostitution. The congregation had no idea of the slavery and secret cruelty so near to their church. When they took note, they changed the lives of innocent young people, and became a voice of conscience in the community. Such was the work of this surprising presence.

There was a shy woman who inherited an unexpected estate from her father and used it to send forty young people to college. Years later, she also set up a foundation to carry on her work upon her death. From her generosity, older women who had never had a chance at an education could return to college and enhance their skills for living. This surprising presence multiplied the works of grace long after her death.

There was a retired engineer who joined his church's overseas mission program, and discovered that thousands of people needed clean drinking water, so he invented a cheaper way of filtering water. The surprising presence gave surprising meaning to the latter part of his life, and saved the lives of thousands of others.

There was a man who did not learn how to read until he was in his forties, but with the encouragement of his pastor, challenged the neighborhood to turn an abandoned building lot filled with debris into a local fruit and vegetable garden. Everyone had a stake, and any food left over was given to those too old or infirm to garden. It was the end of gang violence and the opening of opportunities for many. Neighbors asked him what his motivation was. He told them about that surprising presence, the Spirit of Jesus.

There were people who courageously faced chronic illnesses and found ways of encouraging others, calling on the dying to give assistance and companionship. Through their hearts and hands the surprising presence was made known.

There was a woman who befriended women who had been released from prison, bringing them to church — teaching them about a different Jesus than they had known, and surrounding them with helpful friends. Dozens of women who had been abused found the humanity of God expressed in Jesus conveyed by this woman.

These were some of the stories the retired pastors told, referring to that surprising presence in their ministries. The living Christ had climbed aboard the boats we rowed and inspired us to work with faith, hope, and love.

As we talked, it became clearer that being a pastor presented a variety of challenges and offered us a great joy. We learned skills we thought beyond our capability. We learned to read the Bible with minds that crossed the centuries and spoke of current challenges. We learned to unravel tough organizational problems that had been rusted by rancor. We learned the surprising power of saying little but a simple prayer in the depths of tragedy. We had been touched when someone told us of an unremembered act or a word we said years earlier. We learned patience and resolve when things were not going the way we wanted. We learned to be determined and creative so that the work of Christ's church was not blunted by "we never did things like that before." We learned not to take ourselves too seriously; we trusted that the power of God was more impressive than our abilities. We learned to live with our own humanity, and God used who we were. What was buried in us was a treasure we did not realize we had. God used our humanity, our earthiness, as vessels for the overflowing of love and purpose. We were called upon to grow in faith. We learned to deal with tempers, with discouragement, with times of confusion and doubt, and to be alert to the possibility that the figure on the horizon was indeed real: the Spirit of Jesus, surprising presence. We realized that we were the recipients of surprising springs of generosity and faithful friendship in those we had known. In short, we are grateful we were led to this work and this life. Not only led, but gifted and empowered by the Spirit so that we became people far different from what we were when we started.

As we shared our stories, I thought of my own life as a pastor. At times I might be discouraged, or angry with myself or another person, or exhilarated, or profoundly grateful. In any of these moments, my resource was to turn to the story of Jesus. He is very human to me, and yet filled with the strength of God when confronted with opposition and even death. I said to myself, "He did it: this work we do. He ministered far more deeply and comprehensively than I do, and he turned again and again to God for help. If he did that, so might we." I was convinced that the risen Lord, the living Jesus now ascended to live above all of us, knows our struggles and gives us endurance, courage, and wisdom. It was the Scripture as it told the story of Jesus, and my hope in the overarching care of the risen Lord, that made ministry more than a job — more even than a profession. That surprising presence that met me in Scripture, and in the lives of the faithful, made ministry a life of important challenges, companionship, and hope.

I believe that we who minister are grateful to God as revealed in Jesus Christ, and I hope this book will help others discover both the challenges and the deep satisfactions of being a servant in the church.

DISCUSSION QUESTIONS

1. *What spiritual practices might you participate in that would help you to discern the "surprising presence" of the Lord in your ministry?*

2. *With whom can you honestly share reflections and stories about your ministry?*

3. *Where do you see the Lord at work in your ministry?*

Bibliography

Adams, Arthur Merrihew. *Effective Leadership for Today's Church.* Philadelphia: Westminster, 1978.

Book of Common Prayer, The. New York: Seabury Press, 1979.

Book of Common Worship, The. Philadelphia: Published for the Office of the General Assembly by the General Division of Publication of the Board of Christian Education of the United Presbyterian Church in the United States of America, 1946.

Book of Confessions, The. Part I, *The Constitution of the Presbyterian Church (USA).* Louisville: Office of the General Assembly, Presbyterian Church (USA).

Book of Order, The: The Constitution of the Presbyterian Church (USA). Louisville: Office of the General Assembly, 2009.

Calvin, John, *Institutes of the Christian Religion.* Translated by Henry Beveridge. London: James Clarke and Co., 1953.

————. *Institutes of the Christian Religion.* Translated by Ford Lewis Battles. Philadelphia: Westminster, 1960.

Catholic Encyclopedia. Vol. 2. New York: Robt. Appleton Co., 1907.

Cole, Allan Hugh, Jr., ed. *From Midterms to Ministry: Practical Theologians on Pastoral Beginnings.* Grand Rapids: Eerdmans, 2008.

Conzelmann, Hans. *A Commentary on the First Epistle to the Corinthians.* Philadelphia: Fortress, 1981.

Bibliography

Fisher, B., and W. Ury. *Getting to Yes: Negotiating Agreement without Giving In.* New York: Penguin, 1981.

Guidelines for Session Personnel Committees, Churchwide Personnel Services. Louisville: General Assembly Publications, Presbyterian Church (USA).

Guthrie, Shirley C. *Christian Doctrine.* Rev. ed. Louisville: Westminster John Knox, 1994.

Hall, Douglas John. *God and Human Suffering: An Exercise in the Theology of the Cross.* Minneapolis: Augsburg, 1986.

Heschel, Susannah. *The Aryan Jesus: Christian Theologians and the Bible in Nazi Germany.* Princeton: Princeton University Press, 2008.

Holifield, E. Brooks. *God's Ambassadors: A History of the Christian Clergy in America.* Grand Rapids: Eerdmans, 2007.

Interpreter's Dictionary of the Bible, The. Nashville and New York: Abingdon, 1962.

Jennings, Theodore W., Jr. *Transforming Atonement: A Political Theology of the Cross.* Minneapolis: Fortress, 2009.

Mikoski, Gordon S. *Baptism and Christian Identity.* Grand Rapids: Eerdmans, 2009.

Moltmann, Jürgen. *The Church in the Power of the Spirit: A Contribution to Messianic Theology.* Minneapolis: Fortress, 1993.

"Monday in Ministry." *New Brunswick Presbytery* 2, no. 5 (2006).

Myers, Ched. *Binding the Strong Man.* Maryknoll, N.Y.: Orbis, 1988.

Rediger, G. L. *Clergy Killers.* Louisville: Westminster John Knox, 1997.

Report on Clergy Recruitment and Retention. To the 216th General Assembly (2004) of the Presbyterian Church (USA) Board of Pensions of the Presbyterian Church (USA).

"Sacrament of Baptism, The." In *The Book of Common Worship,* pp. 403-15. Louisville: Westminster John Knox, 1993.

"Theological Understanding of the Relationship between Christians and Jews, A." GA Minutes, 1987, 417-24.

Williamson, Clark M. *A Guest in the House of Israel.* Louisville: Westminster John Knox, 1993.